D0049518

Day by Day

Written by Betty Free • Illustrated by Eira Reeves

TYNDALE
FOR KIDS

Tyndale House Publishers, Inc.
Wheaton, Illinois

Contents

January 1

God, Our Father

We all have the same God and Father. He is over us all.
EPHESIANS 4:6

God made you, and he loves you. God made all the people in the world, so he is like a father to everyone. He is a very special Father. He knows all about you, so he knows what is best for you.

I'm glad that God is the one who is in charge, aren't you? He always knows just what to do.

God is your special Father in heaven. He loves you, and he will take good care of you.

What is God like?

DEAR GOD, thank you for being my special Father in heaven. Thank you for loving me and for knowing how to take care of me. Amen.

January 2

God Will Always Be Around

But the Lord lives on forever. He sits upon his throne. PSALM 9:7

No one but God has always *been* here. No one but God will always *be* here. He lives forever. You can't see him, but he's always with you. And he loves you.

Your mom and dad always love you, but they can't always be with you. They have to go to work, and they need to sleep. But God never has to leave you.

Who will always be with you?

DEAR GOD, I'm glad that you've always been around. And I'm glad that you'll always be right here with me. I love you. Amen.

January 3

Almighty God

I am the Almighty. Obey me and live as you should. GENESIS 17:1

God is very strong. He is more powerful than anyone. He is almighty. So it's no problem for him to take care of us. He can help us when we're sick or sad, and he can keep us safe when we're afraid. All he asks us to do is to obey him. And he even helps us to do that!

Is anyone stronger than God?

THANK YOU, GOD, for using your power to help me. I want to obey you and always do what you want me to do. Amen.

January 4

Valuable Treasure

*Your teachings are
worth more to me than
thousands of pieces of
gold and silver.*
PSALM 119:72

Do you have anything
valuable in your house?
Maybe your mom has some gold
jewelry that is worth a lot of money.
Maybe you have some gold or silver coins.
Sometimes people keep valuable things inside
a treasure chest.

God's Word, the Bible, is like a treasure
chest. Inside are valuable teachings from God.
These teachings show us how to obey him.
They help us learn to love him and to love others.

What do we learn from God's teachings?

DEAR GOD, help me to learn all the
valuable things you teach in the Bible.
Thank you for teaching me how to love
you and others. Amen.

January 5

Learning God's Word

I have stored [your words] in my heart. That way they will hold me back from sin. PSALM 119:11

If you remember the words of a Bible verse, it's like you've put them away. You have them inside your mind, and you have them in your heart, too. That just means that deep down inside where your heart is, the real you wants to do what's right. The words from the Bible help you know what's right. God's words help to keep you from doing bad things that make him sad.

Can you say today's Bible verse?

DEAR GOD, help me to learn many Bible verses.
If I remember your words, I'll know how to do what's right. Amen.

January 6

The Way to Be Wise

Only your rules can give me wisdom and understanding. PSALM 119:104

When you have a question, do you like to know the answer? When you don't understand what you should do, do you like to learn what's right? Parents and teachers can help you learn many things. But the only way they can help you become really wise is by teaching you God's rules. Then you'll understand just how God wants you to live.

How can you become wise?

DEAR GOD, thank you for your rules in the Bible.
They help me understand what's right and what's wrong.
They make me very wise. Amen.

January 7

A Flashlight

*Your words are a lamp to light the
path ahead of me.* PSALM 119:105

Did you ever walk along a path
at night when it was very
dark? It's hard to know where
to walk unless you have a
flashlight, isn't it? You might
stumble and get hurt.

God's words in the Bible are
like a flashlight. If we listen to his
words and obey them, we'll know
where to go and what to do. God
will keep us safe.

**Do you ever wonder what to
do? How can God's Word
help you?**

DEAR GOD, thank you for
wanting me to be safe. Help me
to obey your words in the Bible
so I'll always know where to go
and what to do. Amen.

January 8

God's Light

Your words are a lamp. . . .
They keep me from
stumbling and falling.
PSALM 119:105

A dark room may seem scary. You can't see what's in there. But when you turn on a lamp, the room is light. You can keep from running into toys or stepping on the cat's tail!

God's words are like a lamp. They help us to see different kinds of things clearly. They answer questions like "How should I behave?" or "Would that be a kind thing to say?"

What kinds of things does the Bible help us to see clearly?

DEAR GOD, thank you that your words in the Bible help me to see clearly what to say and do. Amen.

January 9

This Way

*If you go the wrong way . . . you will hear a voice behind you.
It will say, "This is the right way."* ISAIAH 30:21

You've heard your mom say over and over again, "Share your toys." So when you don't do it, you can still hear her voice saying, "Share your toys." Parents don't just teach us what *they* want us to do. They teach us what *God* wants us to do. So listening to them can be like listening to God's voice.

How does God help you know what's right?

DEAR GOD, when I do something wrong, please help me to stop and listen to your voice. Amen.

WRONG WAY

RIGHT WAY

January 10

Ask God

*Teach me to do what you want,
because you are my God.* PSALM 143:10

Sometimes you and your family have to make decisions about what to do. Where should you go to church? Who should you invite to your party? How much money should you spend on new clothes or a new toy? God wants to help you decide. When you talk to him, he will teach you the best way. He will show you how you can make him happy. When you do that, you'll be happy too!

When you need to decide what to do, who is the one you should ask?

DEAR GOD, thank you for helping my family and me know what to do. Amen.

January 11

God's Love

God is love. I JOHN 4:8

How do you know when people love you? Perhaps they tell you, "I love you." But it's even more special when they do something to show love for you. People who love each other give lots of hugs. They do kind things for each other too.

God loves you more than anyone else because he *is* love. He takes care of you, and he answers your prayers. He is a very kind and loving God.

Who loves you more than anyone else?

DEAR GOD, thank you for loving me. Amen.

January 12

Jesus' Love

God . . . made the world through the Son.
The Son . . . is an exact copy of God's nature.
HEBREWS 1:2-3

Children are often a lot like their parents. They look alike and think alike. They even act alike. Maybe you'd like to know what God is like, but he lives in heaven. Well, even before God made the world, his Son, Jesus, was with him. God the Father and God the Son are exactly alike! So you can listen to stories about Jesus' love and know just how much God loves you.

How can you learn about God's love?

DEAR GOD, I'm glad that your Son, Jesus, loves me. And I'm glad that he is just like you. In Jesus' name. Amen.

January 13

Love for All

For God loved the world so much that he gave his only Son.
God gave his Son so that whoever believes in him may not
be lost, but have eternal life. JOHN 3:16

Do you have a pet or a toy that you love very much? It would be hard to give it away or even to let someone else have it for a while.
God gave his Son, Jesus, to us. God let Jesus live in our world for a while. He sent Jesus to take the blame for the bad things we do.
God did this because he loves us so much.

Why did God send his Son, Jesus, to our world?

DEAR GOD, thank you for loving everyone in the world.
Thank you for loving me. I love you, too. Amen.

January 14

A Tiny Bird

Not one sparrow can fall to the ground without your Father knowing it. And what do they cost? You can buy two for a penny! MATTHEW 10:29

God made us and wants us to call him our Father. He made the tiny birds, too. He made a lot of little sparrows and cares about each one.

When Jesus lived on this earth, people could buy two sparrows for a penny. If God cares about tiny birds, you know that he cares about you. Jesus said that you're worth more to God than a lot of sparrows.

Does God care about tiny birds? Does he care about you?

DEAR GOD, thank you for caring about little birds. Thank you for caring about me. Amen.

January 15

Every Hair

*God even knows how many
hairs are on your head.
So don't be afraid.*
MATTHEW 10:30-31

How many hairs do you think you have on your head? There are a lot more than you and your friends could count! Even your mom or dad could never count all your hairs. But God knows how many hairs you have. He knows without even counting! God knows all about you and cares about you very much. He watches over you, so you don't need to be afraid.

Who knows how many hairs you have?

DEAR GOD, I'm glad that you know all about me. I'm glad that you know how to take good care of me. Amen.

January 16

Watching Us Grow

*I, the Lord, will tend the fruitful
vines. Every day I'll water them.
Day and night I'll watch to keep
all enemies away.* ISAIAH 27:3

Did you ever help to plant a
garden? You water the seeds
and watch the leaves begin to grow. You watch to see that no
people or animals walk on your garden. God is like a gardener,
and we're the plants in his garden. He helps us have everything
we need. And he watches over us, keeping us safe as we grow.

How is God like a gardener?

DEAR GOD, thank you for watching over me. Thank you for
keeping me safe as I grow. Amen.

January 17

Don't Be Scared

I am the Lord your God. I am holding your right hand. And I tell you, "Don't be afraid. I will help you." ISAIAH 41:13

Dark bedrooms with flapping curtains. Hairy, frisky spiders. Crashing thunder. There are lots of scary things around! But God is so close to you, it's as if he is holding your hand. He wants to help you when you feel afraid. He wants you to tell him how you feel.

What should you remember when you feel scared?

DEAR GOD, you know what scares me. Thank you for being with me to listen and to help me when I'm afraid. Amen.

January 18

Help!

Call to me in times of trouble. I will save you.
PSALM 50:15

If you fall down and hurt your knee, you probably call out to whoever is close by. You call for the person who is taking care of you. But who do you think helps that person hear you? Who helps that person know what to do? God does! You can call to God anytime—even when no one else is around. If you're sad or afraid or hurt, God can help you.

Who is the one you can always call to when you need help?

DEAR GOD, thank you for showing my mom and dad and other people how to help me. I'm glad that I can call to you at any time. Amen.

January 19

Come to Me

*Come to me, all of you
who are tired and have
heavy loads. I will give
you rest.*
MATTHEW 11:28

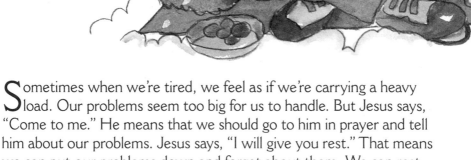

Sometimes when we're tired, we feel as if we're carrying a heavy load. Our problems seem too big for us to handle. But Jesus says, "Come to me." He means that we should go to him in prayer and tell him about our problems. Jesus says, "I will give you rest." That means we can put our problems down and forget about them. We can rest and trust Jesus to take care of us.

What should you do when you have a problem?

DEAR LORD, thank you for letting me talk to you about my problems. Help me to trust you to take care of them. Amen.

January 20

Strange Places

The Lord answered, "I myself will go with you." EXODUS 33:14

Moses had to take a big crowd of people across a desert to a new country. Moses wasn't sure that he could do it. But God said, "I myself will go with you." What a great promise! That promise is for kids like you, too. Where do you think the children in the pictures need to go? To the doctor? To a new house? God will go with them. And he'll go with you wherever you go.

Name some places where God will go with you.

DEAR GOD, sometimes I don't like to go to new places. Thank you for going with me. Amen.

January 21

A Safe Place

Those who listen to me will live in safety. They will be safe, without fear of being hurt. PROVERBS 1:33

If you want to be really, really safe, where do you go? Maybe you run into your mom's or dad's arms. You do that because you know they love you and they can protect you. Another way to be really, really safe is to listen to God. You can listen to his words in the Bible. Then you'll know how to trust him and obey him. He will take very good care of you.

What should you do when you want to be sure that you'll be safe?

DEAR GOD, help me to know that I can always feel safe when I listen to you and obey you. Amen.

January 22

On Guard!

The Lord is faithful. He will
make you strong and guard you.
2 THESSALONIANS 3:3

Kings, queens, presidents, and other important people have helpers who guard them and keep them safe. You are important, too. You are very important to God, so he guards you and protects you from bad things. He even makes you strong enough to handle bad things that happen by yourself.

Sometimes you might feel sad, but God will help you trust him. He is faithful. That means you can always count on him to be there to help.

What will God do when you need help?

DEAR GOD, thank you that I can always count on your help. In Jesus' name. Amen.

January 23

All the Time

*I am trusting you,
O Lord. . . . My times
are in your hands.*
PSALM 31:14-15

What time is it? Is it early in the morning? Is it late in the afternoon or evening? No matter what time it is, you can say, "I am trusting you, O Lord."

The Lord our God is with us all the time. He is with us in good times and bad times. Everything is in his hands. That means he is in charge and will take care of things all the time.

Name times when God will take care of you.

DEAR GOD, thank you for taking care of everything all through the day and all through the night, too. Amen.

January 24

Comfort from God

*[God] comforts
us every time we
have trouble.*
2 CORINTHIANS 1:4

When you feel sad or upset, you need someone to comfort you and make you feel better. God will do that for you. Sometimes he sends a person from your family to help you feel better. Sometimes he comforts you as you hold on to a favorite doll or stuffed animal. Even when you think you're all alone, God is with you. You can always talk to him, and he'll comfort you every time.

When do you need to be comforted?

DEAR GOD, thank you for knowing when I need to be comforted. Thank you for all the times when you have helped me feel better. Amen.

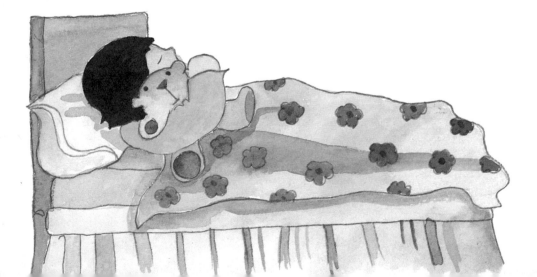

January 25

Free from Worries

Give all your worries to [God], because he cares for you. I PETER 5:7

People worry a lot. Grown-ups worry about getting sick or not having enough money. Kids worry about not having enough time with Mom and Dad or not getting along with friends. But God doesn't want you to worry. He wants you to talk to him about the things that bother you and then trust him to help you. He'll take care of you because he cares about you.

Why don't you need to worry about anything?

DEAR GOD, thank you for listening when I tell you about the things that bother me. Thank you for caring about me. I love you. Amen.

January 26

A Mother Hen

He will protect you like a bird spreading its wings over its young.
PSALM 91:4

A mother hen is a big bird that flutters about and gathers her little chicks under her wings. She wants them to be safe and warm. That's how God feels about you. He wants to protect you. You can run to God the way a little chick runs to its mother! Praying is like running to God. Listening to God's words in the Bible is like running to him too.

How is God like a mother bird?

DEAR GOD, thank you for keeping me safe under your wings. I want to talk to you and listen to your words in the Bible. Amen.

January 27

Counting Sheep

*The Lord gives sleep
to those he loves.*
PSALM 127:2

Have you ever felt like the little girl in the picture? Are there times when you just can't sleep? Maybe you toss and turn. You count sheep. You ask your mom for a drink of water. Do you know what else you can do? You can pray! The Bible says that sleep is a gift from God. So all you have to do is tell him you'd like to receive his gift, and he'll give it to you.

What will you do the next time you can't sleep?

DEAR LORD, you know how tired I get when I've been playing all day. When I go to bed, I'll trust you to give me a good night's rest. Amen.

January 28

Broken Hearts

He heals the brokenhearted.
He bandages their wounds.
PSALM 147:3

If one of your toys gets broken,
someone might be able to fix it.
If you get hurt, someone might
help by putting a bandage on the hurt place.

When a person feels very, very sad, it's as
if something is broken or hurt inside. We say that the person's heart
is broken. But no ordinary bandage will help! Only God can fix
a broken heart. You can talk to him, and he'll help you.

When do you feel sad? Who can help you then?

DEAR GOD, thank you for friends who pray for me when I'm sad.
Thank you for fixing my heart when it feels as if it is broken.
In Jesus' name. Amen.

January 29

God on His Throne

I saw the Lord. He was sitting on a very high throne. His long robe filled the Temple.
ISAIAH 6:1

God let a man named Isaiah see what heaven is like. Isaiah tells us that he saw the Lord God sitting on a throne, as the King. Bright heavenly creatures were singing happy songs of praise to God. They sang, "Holy, holy, holy is the Lord." They called him holy because he is perfect and good. He could never do anything bad. No one but God is holy.

What happy songs of praise do you like to sing to God?

DEAR LORD, I praise you for being perfect and good. There is no one like you, God! Amen.

January 30

Like a Rainbow

On the throne was a shape like a man. . . . I saw a bright light all around him. The glow around him looked like the rainbow in the clouds on a rainy day.
EZEKIEL 1:26-28

A man named Ezekiel saw a bright light around God. It looked like a rainbow with many different colors. When you look at a rainbow, you can think about how special God is. No one but God sits on a throne in heaven. No one else has a bright light around him that looks like a rainbow.

Will you think about God when you see a rainbow? Why?

DEAR GOD, I praise you for being so special. Thank you for rainbows that remind us of you. Amen.

January 31

We'll Know!

*[Jesus prayed,] "Then the world will know
you sent me. And the world will understand
that you love them as much as you love me."*
JOHN 17:23

God's Son, Jesus, prayed that we would
know about God's love. God sits on a
throne in heaven, but he wants us to
understand what he is like. So he sent
Jesus. God loves his Son. But God also
loves you and me and everyone else just as
much. Learning about Jesus from the Bible helps
us to understand God's love.

**Name some people God loves just as much
as he loves his own Son, Jesus.**

DEAR GOD, I praise you for your love. I'm very happy that you
love me. I love you, too. In Jesus' name. Amen.

February 1

When Time Began

God said, "Let there be light!" And there was light. GENESIS 1:3

Way back at the beginning of time, God made the earth. There were no people or animals yet. There weren't any trees or bushes. There wasn't even any dry land. The earth was empty and dark.

Then God said that there should be light, and there it was! God looked at the light, and he knew it was good. He named it "day." But God still wanted it to be dark part of the time. He called the darkness "night."

All of this happened on day one.

What do you like to do when it's light?
What do you like to do when it's dark?

DEAR GOD, thank you for making light so I can see how to do lots of things. Thank you for the darkness, too. I can keep my eyes closed and get lots of rest when it's dark. You know just what I need! Amen.

February 2

The Water and the Sky

God named the air "sky." GENESIS 1:8

When God first made the earth, there was water all over it, but there was no air above. God knew he was going to make birds that would need air to fly through. He knew he was going to make animals and people who would need air to breathe. So, on the second day, God put air all around the earth. He called the air "sky," and he saw that it was good. God was very wise to make the air.

Why did God make the sky?

DEAR GOD, thank you for the beautiful blue sky up above. Thank you for knowing what your world needs. Amen.

February 3

Seas and Trees

The earth produced plants. . . . The trees made fruit with seeds in it. . . . God saw that all this was good. GENESIS 1:12

On day three God said the water should come together so there would be dry ground. God called the dry part "earth" and the wet part "seas." Then God told the earth to make plants—grass and trees and bushes. He gave each plant seeds that could grow and make more plants. Everything God did was good.

What can you do on the land? in the water?

DEAR GOD, Thank you for water and land. Thank you for green grass and tall trees. Thanks for plants with beautiful flowers and good fruit, too. Amen.

February 4

Lights in the Sky

God had made two huge lights, the sun and moon, to shine down upon the earth. . . . He had also made the stars. GENESIS 1:16

On day four God did something else good. He put the sun in the sky to shine during the day. He put the moon and stars in the sky to shine at night. Now each time the sun came up, it would be a new day. Each time there was a new moon, it would be a new month. And every three months there would be a new season: spring, summer, fall, or winter.

What time of the day do you like the best?

DEAR GOD, thank you for sunshine and for twinkling stars. Thank you for every new day! Amen.

February 5

Wings and Fins

God said, "Let the water be filled with living things. And let birds fly in the air above the earth." GENESIS 1:20

On day five God told the water to be filled with big fish, little fish, and other sea creatures such as crabs and dolphins. God also made birds to fly in the air. He made big eagles, tiny chickadees, red birds, blue birds, and yellow birds. God told the fish to have young ones. He told the birds to have babies, too. And God saw that it was all good.

Can you pretend to swim like a fish and fly like a bird?

DEAR GOD, thank you for making fish and birds. Amen.

February 6

Animals and People

God said, "Let the earth be filled with animals."
Then God said, "Let us make human beings."
GENESIS 1:24, 26

On day six God made animals—big elephants and tiny bugs, soft rabbits and prickly porcupines. Then God made the most special creatures of all. He made a man and a woman! God made people to be like himself. He told them to have children and to take good care of the whole world. God looked at everything he had made and saw that it was very good.

How can you be kind to an animal?
Can you take care of a plant?

DEAR GOD, thank you for making me! Help me to take good care of your world. Amen.

February 7

A Day to Rest

God blessed the seventh day and made it a holy day. He made it holy because on that day he rested. GENESIS 2:3

God finished all of his work in six days. So on day seven God rested. He made that day a special, holy day for his people, too. For a long time, God's people rested on the seventh day of every week. Then God's Son, Jesus, died and came alive again on the first day of the week. Since that time, God's people usually rest and worship him on the first day of every week.

What do you like to do on God's special day?

DEAR GOD, I'm glad you took a day to rest. I'm glad you made one day each week special for everyone. Amen.

February 8

I Praise You, God

Lord, you have made many things.
With your wisdom you made them all.
I will sing praises to my God as long as I live.
PSALM 104:24, 33

God can make many wonderful things because he is such a great and wonderful God. No one has as much wisdom as he does. That means God is very wise and knows how to make everything. He sends sunshine and rain so fields and fruit trees keep growing and everyone can have food to eat. Let's praise God and tell him we know how great he is!

Why should we praise God?

DEAR GOD, I praise you for all the wonderful things you've made. You are a great God! Amen.

February 9

It's God's World!

*The earth and everything in it belong
to the Lord. The world and all its
people belong to him.* PSALM 24:1

When you make something,
it belongs to you, doesn't it?
Nobody else can make it exactly like you.
Well, God made the world, so it belongs to
him. He made us, so we belong to him too!
God loves us so much that he wants us to
enjoy the world. He didn't make the
world just for himself. He made it for
you and for me. Isn't God wonderful?

**Who is it that the world
belongs to?**

DEAR GOD, thank you for sharing your world with me. Thank you
for helping me paint pretty pictures of your world. Amen.

February 10

Why Does God Care?

*I look at the heavens. . . . I see the moon
and stars, which you created. But why
is man important to you? Why do you
take care of human beings?*
PSALM 8:3-4

Did you ever look up at the moon and stars and
think about how far away they are? Did you ever try to
count the stars? God must be pretty great to have made
the whole sky with so many things in it.

We can't help but wonder why such a great God cares about people.
Are we really important to him? Yes, we are. God says so himself! And he
shows that he cares about people by all the wonderful things he does for us.

Are you important to God? How do you know?

DEAR GOD, I know you made
all the stars and many more
things in the sky. I'm glad you
also love and care for me.
Amen.

February 11

What's in a Name?

*[Mary] will give birth to a son.
You will name the son Jesus . . .
because he will save his people
from their sins.* MATTHEW 1:21

A long time after God made the world, he made some special plans. He wanted people to know how much he really loved them. So he planned to send his own Son to the world. The baby would be in Mary and Joseph's family. An angel told Joseph to name the child Jesus. His name means "the Lord saves." He wants to save us from our sins. Sins are the bad things we do.

Did you celebrate Jesus' birth last Christmas? What does his name mean?

DEAR GOD, thank you for sending Jesus to save us from the bad things we do. Amen.

February 12

Follow the Leader

"Are you the Christ, the Son of the blessed God?"
Jesus answered, "I am." MARK 14:61-62

Jesus is sometimes called the "Christ" or "Jesus Christ." This title means "the great leader God has sent to save his people."

Countries have leaders too. In some countries the leader's title is "president." In other places the leader is called the "king" or "queen." But no leader is like Jesus Christ. He is God, and only he can save us from the bad things we do.

Why is Jesus Christ such a good leader?

DEAR GOD, thank you for sending your Son to be my leader. I pray this in the name of Jesus Christ. Amen.

February 13

A New Name

*It was there at Antioch
that the believers were
first called "Christians."*
ACTS 11:26

When Jesus lived on this earth, many people followed him wherever he went. And many of those people believed that he was God's Son. After Jesus went back to heaven, even more people began to believe in him. Some of these believers lived in Antioch. That's where they were first called Christians.

A Christian loves and obeys God's Son, Jesus Christ.

What does a Christian believe about Jesus?

DEAR JESUS, thank you that I can believe in you. Help me to love and obey you. I pray this in your name. Amen.

February 14

A Very Good Shepherd

[Jesus said,] "I am the good shepherd." JOHN 10:11

Jesus wanted us to know that he loves us and will take very good care of us. So he gave himself a special name, "the good shepherd." In Bible times a shepherd walked ahead of his sheep, and they followed him. He led his sheep to fields of green grass, and he kept them safe from wild animals. Jesus is like a shepherd, and we're like sheep. Jesus takes good care of us.

Why does Jesus call himself "the good shepherd"?

DEAR JESUS, thank you for being my shepherd. Thank you for letting me be your little lamb. Amen.

February 15

Father and Son

[God's] voice said, "This is my Son and I love him. I am very pleased with him."
MATTHEW 3:17

Think about how happy it makes you feel when your mom and dad say nice things about you. Jesus also must have felt happy when his Father in heaven said nice things about him. Jesus had just been baptized in a river to show that he belonged to God. He went down into the water and came back up again. Then God, his heavenly Father, said he loved Jesus and was pleased with him.

How did God say he felt about his Son, Jesus?

DEAR GOD, thank you for my family. Thank you that we can all belong to you, just like your Son, Jesus, does. Amen.

February 16

God's Children

The Father . . . loved us so much that we are called children of God. And we really are his children. 1 JOHN 3:1

Mom, Dad, sisters, brothers, aunts, uncles, cousins, grandparents—what big families some people have! God loves us so much that he wants all of us to be in his big family! To help us join his family, God sent his Son, Jesus, to save us. All people who loved Jesus in the past and all people who love him now are called God's children.

What does God call everyone who loves Jesus?

DEAR GOD, I'm glad you have a big family and that you want me to be your child. Amen.

February 17

Belonging

Some people did accept him. They believed in him. To them [Jesus] gave the right to become children of God.
JOHN 1:12

The people you live with are your family. They love you, and you belong to them. You can become part of God's family too. To do that, you need to believe that Jesus is God's Son. You need to accept him as the only one who can save you from the bad things you do. Jesus wants you to be God's child. He wants you to be part of God's family.

Whose family does Jesus want you to join?

DEAR JESUS, thank you for wanting me in God's family. Help me to believe in you. Amen.

February 18

Brothers and Sisters

[Jesus said,] "My true brothers and sisters and mother are those who do the things that my Father in heaven wants." MATTHEW 12:50

When Jesus lived on earth, he had a family. He lived with his mother, Mary, and her husband, Joseph, who was like a father to him. But Jesus' real Father is God, who lives in heaven. So Jesus' real family is God's family. Children and grown-ups who love God and obey him are brothers and sisters to Jesus.

How can you be a brother or sister to Jesus?

DEAR GOD, I love you. Help me to learn what you want me to do. Thank you that I can be in the same family as you and your Son, Jesus. Amen.

February 19

Sweet Words

*Your promises are so sweet to me.
They are like honey to my mouth!*
PSALM 119:103

Your body needs to grow strong, so your mom or dad must give you food. Your love for God needs to grow strong too. You need to know that God is a kind Father who has promised to love and care for you. When you hear his promises, it's like eating sweet honey or cookies or cake. Isn't it wonderful to have a Father in heaven who makes promises like that?

What does your Father in heaven promise to do?

DEAR GOD, I want to learn all about your sweet promises in the Bible. Then I can love you even more! Amen.

February 20

Everyone Is Special

You are all the same in Christ Jesus.
GALATIANS 3:28

People are different in many ways. Some are tall, and some are short. Some have brown eyes; some have blue. Some are teachers, and some are students. Some are boys; some are girls.

But the Bible says that all people who love Jesus are the same. They may look different on the outside. But to God, they are all alike. They are all special to him, and he loves everyone just the same. He loves everyone just as much as he loves his own Son, Jesus.

If people look different, how can they still be the same?

DEAR GOD, thank you for all of the different people in your family. Thank you for loving everyone the same. Help me to do that too. Amen.

February 21

Angels on a Ladder

Jacob dreamed that there was a ladder . . . reaching up into heaven. And he saw angels of God going up and coming down the ladder. GENESIS 28:12

Jacob was sleeping alone outside. But God let him know that he wasn't really alone by sending him a special dream. God let Jacob see angels! God made many angels. They worship him in heaven. They also come to earth, but most of the time we can't see them. Sometimes God sends them with special messages. And he often sends them to protect us.

What are some things that angels do?

DEAR GOD, thank you for making angels and for taking good care of me. Amen.

February 22

An Angel with a Message

Last night an angel stood beside me. . . . He said, "Don't be afraid, Paul." ACTS 27:23-24

Paul was on a boat one time when a bad storm came up. The other men were afraid, but Paul told them they didn't need to be. He told them that God had sent an angel with a special message. All of them were going to be OK! Wasn't God good to send an angel to Paul with that message?

Who brought a message from God to Paul? Do you remember a message that angels brought to some shepherds?

DEAR GOD, thank you for sending angels with special messages. I'm glad the Bible tells us about your angels. Amen.

February 23

An Army of Angels

The Lord opened the eyes of the young man. And he saw that the mountain was full of horses and chariots of fire all around Elisha.
2 KINGS 6:17

You can't see God. And you usually can't see angels. But God sends them to help keep you safe. He may send one angel or lots of them. One time an enemy army was attacking a city. Elisha's helper was afraid. Then God let the young man see the angels. They came as soldiers, and they were everywhere! They kept Elisha and his helper safe.

When might God send angels to keep you safe?

DEAR GOD, I can't see you or your angels. But I'm glad that you are with me and that you send your angels to keep me safe. Amen.

February 24

A Donkey Sees an Angel

The donkey saw the angel of the Lord standing in the road.
The angel had a sword in his hand. NUMBERS 22:23

A man named Balaam was riding along a country road when an angel blocked his way. He couldn't see the angel, but his donkey could. The donkey went off the path three times so he wouldn't run into the angel. Balaam hit his donkey. Finally Balaam also saw the angel, who had a message from God. Balaam obeyed, and God kept him safe. Then Balaam knew he had one smart donkey!

How did Balaam's donkey help him?

DEAR GOD, thank you for helping us know where to go. Thank you for angels that block the paths we shouldn't take. Amen.

February 25

Ordinary People

Some people have . . . welcomed angels without knowing it.
HEBREWS 13:2

M ost of the time we can't see angels. Sometimes they have a bright light around them. But once in a while angels look like ordinary people. One time Abraham saw three men coming toward his tent. He didn't know them, but he welcomed them and gave them a meal. It turned out that they were angels. They said God was going to give Abraham and his wife a son!

What did Abraham do for the three strangers?

THANK YOU, GOD, for angels and for ordinary people. Show me how to be friendly, especially to new kids in my neighborhood. Amen.

February 26

The Lions' Den

Daniel answered, ". . . My God sent his angel to close the lions' mouths. They have not hurt me."
DANIEL 6:21-22

Daniel loved God. He prayed to God three times every day. Some men who did not love God didn't like Daniel either. They threw Daniel into a den full of mean, hungry lions. But Daniel trusted God to take care of him, and he did! God sent an angel. The angel closed the lions' mouths so they couldn't hurt Daniel one bit.

How did God help Daniel?

I LOVE YOU, GOD, just like Daniel did. I don't see any lions, but I know you can keep me safe from anything! Thanks, God. Amen.

February 27

Out of Jail

Suddenly there was a light . . . ! And an Angel of the Lord stood beside Peter!
ACTS 12:7

Peter liked to preach about Jesus, but some people didn't want Peter to do that. So they threw him in jail. They put chains on him and placed him between two guards. While some friends were praying for Peter that night, an angel came and woke him. The chains fell off, and Peter followed the angel. Then the jail doors opened. The angel left, but Peter was safe!

Who prayed for Peter? How did God answer their prayer?

DEAR GOD, please send your angels to help everyone who wants to tell others about your Son, Jesus. Amen.

February 28

Food in the Desert

Elijah lay down under the tree and slept. Suddenly an angel came to him and touched him. The angel said, "Get up and eat."
1 KINGS 19:5

Elijah was sad. He was afraid, too. A wicked queen was planning to kill him. Elijah ran away to a hot, dry desert. He fell asleep feeling hungry and alone. Then God sent an angel to cheer him up! The angel said he should eat. When Elijah looked around, he saw a loaf of hot bread and a jar of water. So he ate and drank. Then he felt better.

**Name some times when you need to be cheered up.
How might God help?**

DEAR GOD, I'm glad that angels can cheer people up when they're tired or sad. Amen.

February 29

Angels Everywhere

He has put his angels in charge of you.
They will watch over you wherever
you go. PSALM 91:11

God's angels helped Bible people,
and they can help you. Do
you know who gives all the
angels their orders? God does!
He tells them where to go and
how to help people.

God loves you and wants you to be safe. He goes with you
wherever you go. He tells his angels to go with you also. He tells
them to keep you safe.

Where will you go today? tomorrow? Can God's angels
protect you wherever you go?

DEAR GOD, thank you for ordering your angels
to keep me safe. Help me to always trust you.
In Jesus' name. Amen.

March 1

A Special Trip

When Jesus was 12 years old he went with his parents to Jerusalem. They traveled there for the yearly Passover Feast. LUKE 2:41-42

When Jesus was growing up, people who loved God went to the city of Jerusalem each year. They went there to worship God at the temple. The temple was like a big, beautiful church. Jesus and his family and their friends walked for a long time. They were excited about going to the temple.

Have you ever gone to a special place to worship God? (Maybe you were on vacation or in a big city.)

THANK YOU, GOD, for special places where I can pray and sing to you with my family and friends. Amen.

March 2

Lost!

*After the feast was over . . . Jesus stayed
behind in Jerusalem. His parents . . .
thought he was with friends . . . .
But then he didn't show up that evening.
So they started to look for him.* LUKE 2:43-44

H ow do you think Mary and Joseph felt
when they couldn't find Jesus? Were they
afraid? upset?

Parents want to take good care of their
children. That's why your mom wants to
hold your hand when you go somewhere.
That's why your parents ask someone they
trust to stay with you when they need to
go away.

How do your parents make sure you are safe?

DEAR GOD, thank you that
my family cares about me
and wants to know that
I'm safe. Amen.

March 3

Found!

[Jesus] was in the Temple,
sitting among the teachers of the
Law. He was talking about deep
questions with them. And he
amazed everyone with his answers.
LUKE 2:46-47

At last Mary and Joseph found Jesus. He was at the temple, talking with teachers about God's laws. Even though Jesus was only 12 years old, he knew a lot about God's laws. That's because he is God's Son. But the teachers didn't know that. They were surprised at how much he knew.

What did Jesus talk about at the temple?

DEAR GOD, thank you for teachers who help me know all about you and your laws. Thank you for everyone who reads Bible stories to me. In Jesus' name. Amen.

JESUS

March 4

Worried Parents

*"Son!" [Jesus'] mother said to him.
". . . Your father and I have been . . . looking
for you everywhere!" "But why did you
need to look?" he asked.* LUKE 2:48-49

M ary and Joseph were worried about Jesus.
They didn't know that he was safe at the
temple. They had to look many places before
they found him.

Jesus wasn't trying to hide, and he didn't
want his family to be afraid or upset. He thought
Mary and Joseph would know where he was.

**Why were Mary and Joseph worried? Can you name a time
when your parents were worried about you?**

DEAR GOD, thank you for my family.
Help me not to make them worry.
Amen.

March 5

A Special Father

"Why did you need to look?" [Jesus] asked. "Didn't you know that I would be here at the Temple, in my Father's House?" LUKE 2:49

Jesus knew some things about himself that no one else understood. He knew that his family loved him and took good care of him. But he also knew that his real Father was God.

The big, beautiful temple where people went to worship God was called "God's house." So Jesus called it his "Father's House." Jesus loved his heavenly Father and wanted to spend time at his house.

Why did Jesus like to be at the temple?

DEAR GOD, I'm glad that I can worship you at my church and learn to obey you. I can learn to be kind and help people. Amen.

March 6

Learning Days

[Jesus] went back to Nazareth with them and obeyed them. . . . Jesus grew both tall and wise. LUKE 2:51-52

Jesus went back home with Mary and Joseph to the town of Nazareth. That's where Jesus grew up. He helped his family and did what they asked him to do. He probably got water from a well for his mother and helped Joseph in the carpenter shop. He grew tall, and he grew wise. He always knew what was right to do, and that's what he did!

In what ways did Jesus grow?

DEAR GOD, help me grow up to be like your Son, Jesus. Show me how to help my family and learn from them. Amen.

March 7

Twelve Special Friends

Jesus chose 12 men and called them apostles. He wanted these 12 to be with him, and he wanted to send them to other places to preach. MARK 3:14

Jesus grew up and began teaching people about God. He wanted others to teach people too. So he chose 12 special friends to follow him and learn from him. He chose Peter, James, and John. He chose Andrew, Philip, and Bartholomew. He also chose Matthew, Thomas, and another man named James. He chose Thaddaeus, Simon, and Judas, too. These men learned from Jesus so they could tell others about him.

What did Jesus want his special helpers to do?

DEAR GOD, I want to learn from your Son, Jesus, too. Help me to learn how to teach people about you. In Jesus' name. Amen.

March 8

The Happy People

Jesus taught the people and said: "Those who want to do right more than anything else are happy. Those who work to bring peace are happy."
MATTHEW 5:2, 6, 9

One day Jesus sat down on a hillside and told his friends how to be happy. He said people are happy when they know they need God's help. They're happy when doing what is right is what's most important to them. They're happy when they are kind and when they want to help others get along together.

What are some things you can do to be happy?

DEAR GOD, I'm glad your Son taught us how to be happy. In Jesus' name. Amen.

March 9

Let the Children Come

Some people brought their small children to Jesus. . . . But his followers told the people to stop. . . . When Jesus saw this, he . . . said to them, "Let the little children come to me. Don't stop them." MARK 10:13-14

Jesus' helpers thought he would not want to be bothered with little children. They were wrong! Jesus loved the children and wanted to see them.

Maybe you have a grandpa, a grandma, or a friend who is never too busy for you. Does that person hug you and listen to you and pray for you? Then you know what Jesus is like!

How does Jesus feel about children?

DEAR JESUS, I'm glad you love me. I love you, too. In your name I pray. Amen.

March 10

Dinner Is Ready

Jesus touched her hand, and the fever left her.
MATTHEW 8:15

Peter's wife was sad because her mother was very sick. Her mother was in bed and had a high fever. Then Jesus came to visit. He saw how sick the woman was. Jesus wanted to help her, and he knew he could. He just touched her hand, and she was well again! She didn't even have to stay in bed. She got up right away and cooked dinner!

How did Jesus help the woman who had a fever?

DEAR JESUS, thank you for caring about sick people. I know you can help my friends when they're sick. Thank you for helping me, too. Amen.

March 11

Don't Be Afraid

When Jesus heard this, he said to Jairus, "Don't be afraid. Just believe, and your daughter will be well."
LUKE 8:50

A man named Jairus had a little girl who was very sick. He asked Jesus to help her. But the little girl was so sick that she died. Jesus told her dad not to be afraid. He wanted her dad to know that he could still help. Jesus went home with the man and brought the little girl back to life. Her parents were surprised—and very happy!

Why didn't Jairus need to be afraid?

DEAR JESUS, thank you that I can trust you when I'm sick. Help my family to trust you too. Amen.

March 12

Love Your Neighbor

So he said to Jesus, "And who is my neighbor?" LUKE 10:29

Jesus told a story about a man who needed help. Robbers had taken his money and had hurt him. Two people came by, but they didn't stop. Then a man from far away came along. He covered up the man's hurt places. And he took the hurt man to an inn, where he could stay and get well. Jesus said that people who need help are our neighbors. We should be like the man who stopped to help.

Can you think of someone who needs your help?

DEAR GOD, show me how to love my neighbors—even the ones who aren't nice to me. In Jesus' name. Amen.

March 13

The Lost Sheep

Be happy with me because I found my lost sheep! LUKE 15:6

Jesus told a story about a man who had 100 sheep, but one of them was lost. He hunted everywhere until he found it. The man was so happy! He picked up the little sheep and carried it home on his shoulders. Then he called his friends and had a party.

Jesus loves you even more than this man loved his sheep! Jesus takes good care of you.

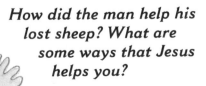

How did the man help his lost sheep? What are some ways that Jesus helps you?

DEAR JESUS, I'm like your little sheep. I know you love me very much. Thank you. Amen.

March 14

A Tiny Seed

*The kingdom of heaven is like a mustard seed. . . .
That seed is the smallest of all seeds. But when
it grows, it . . . becomes a tree, big enough for
the wild birds to come and make nests in its
branches.* MATTHEW 13:31-32

Did you ever plant a little seed? Did you water it
and wait for it to grow? A tiny mustard seed
grows into a big tree like the one in the picture. God's
family started out like a little seed. But his family has
grown big like the tree. All of the people who love
Jesus and obey him belong to the kingdom of heaven.

How can you become part of the growing kingdom of heaven?

DEAR GOD, thank you for your Son, Jesus. I'm glad he
came to help me become part of your kingdom. Amen.

March 15

A Storm

Jesus stood up and . . . said, "Quiet! Be still!" Then the wind stopped, and the lake became calm. MARK 4:39

Jesus was sleeping in a boat when a storm came up. The wind blew hard, and water began coming into the boat. Jesus' friends were afraid. They woke Jesus up and shouted, "We're drowning!" Jesus told the storm to stop. Then he asked his friends why they were afraid. He wanted them to trust him.

How did Jesus help his friends during a storm?

DEAR JESUS, thank you for being with me during storms and other times when I'm afraid. Help me to trust you. Amen.

March 16

Food for Everyone

Here is a boy with five loaves of barley bread and two little fish.
JOHN 6:9

All day, more than 5,000 people had been listening to Jesus teach about God. Now they were hungry and tired. There was no town and no food nearby. But one young boy let Jesus have his lunch. Jesus took that little bit of food and turned it into a lot of food. He fed all of the people.

How many people did Jesus feed with one little lunch?

DEAR JESUS, thank you for all the special things that you can do. Thank you for giving me enough food to eat each day. Amen.

March 17

Knock, Knock! Who's There?

Keep on asking and you will keep on getting. LUKE 11:9

Jesus said to pretend a person came to visit late at night. You had no bread, so you went to a friend's house. He didn't want to get up. But you kept knocking on the door until he came and gave you bread.

Jesus said that when we pray, we should keep on asking for the things we need. We shouldn't give up if God doesn't seem to answer right away.

Do you need bread to eat? clothes to wear? What else do you need? Can you talk to God about it?

DEAR GOD, thank you for letting me keep on talking to you. I'm glad you'll give me what I need at the right time. In Jesus' name. Amen.

March 18

Hooray for Jesus!

The crowd in Jerusalem heard that Jesus was coming. . . . They took palm branches and waved them.
JOHN 12:12-13

It was time to go into the city of Jerusalem. Jesus asked two friends to bring him a young donkey that he could ride into the city. Many people went out to meet Jesus. They walked along the road with him. It was like a parade! People waved palm branches and shouted praises to God.

Every year we celebrate this day at church. We call it Palm Sunday.

How did Jesus' friends welcome him?

DEAR JESUS, I would like to have waved a palm branch when you rode on a donkey. But I can still praise you and tell you that I love you. Amen.

March 19

A Long Night

All the leading priests and older leaders of the people decided to kill Jesus. They . . . led him away. MATTHEW 27:1-2

Four days after Jesus rode into Jerusalem on a donkey, he ate a special supper with his helpers. Then he went to a garden with them to pray. He knew sad things would happen soon, and they did. Men with swords and clubs took Jesus away. The next morning, some leaders decided to kill Jesus. He loved us so much that he didn't run away. He was willing to die for our sins.

Why didn't Jesus run away?

DEAR JESUS, I feel sad when I think about what people did to you. You let them do it because you love everyone so much. Thank you. Amen.

March 20

On a Wooden Cross

The soldiers nailed Jesus to his cross. . . . Jesus said, "Father, forgive them. They don't know what they are doing."
LUKE 23:33-34

Jesus' enemies wanted him to be killed. They had him put on a big cross made from two pieces of wood. But Jesus wasn't angry with them. He asked God to forgive them. He stayed on the cross and died there so that everyone's sins could be forgiven. His friends were sad. They didn't think they would ever see him again after that Friday. But they were in for a big surprise!

Why did Jesus stay on the cross?

DEAR JESUS, thank you for dying so that everyone's sins can be forgiven. Amen.

March 21

The Tomb

[Joseph] put Jesus' body in a new tomb. An angel . . . went to the tomb and rolled the stone away. The soldiers guarding the tomb were very frightened.

MATTHEW 27:60; 28:2, 4

Soldiers were watching the cave, or tomb, where a friend had put Jesus' body. Early on Sunday morning, the earth shook and an angel came down from heaven. The angel rolled away the stone that was in front of the tomb. The soldiers were scared. Jesus was gone!

Who do you see in the tomb?

DEAR GOD, I'm glad that Jesus didn't stay in the tomb. Thank you for bringing him back to life. Amen.

March 22

A Wonderful Surprise

The angel spoke to the women. "Don't be afraid!" he said. "I know you are looking for Jesus. . . . But he isn't here! For he has come back to life again."
MATTHEW 28:5-6

Some women were awake early on Sunday morning. They were sad as they walked to the tomb. But what a wonderful surprise was waiting for them! An angel was in the tomb. He said that Jesus was alive again! He told the women to hurry and tell Jesus' helpers the good news.

Every year we celebrate this day at church. We call it Easter.

What news did the angel have?

DEAR GOD, help me to share the good news about Jesus with my family and my friends. Amen.

March 23

A Special Visitor

As they sat down to eat, he asked God's blessing on the food.
Then he took a small loaf of bread. He broke it and passed it over
to them. LUKE 24:30

It was Sunday evening. Jesus had just come back to life that morning. Two of his friends were walking along a road. They were sad because they didn't believe that Jesus was alive. Jesus came and walked with them, but they couldn't tell who he was. He told them what God's Book said about himself. They liked what he said and asked him to stay with them. When they ate together, they knew who he was!

Who was the special visitor?

DEAR JESUS, I know you are alive, so I don't have to be sad. I love you! Amen.

March 24

Some Fish for Jesus

Jesus . . . said to them, "Peace be with you." They gave him a piece of cooked fish. While the followers watched, Jesus took the fish and ate it. LUKE 24:36, 42-43

Jesus' helpers were together in an upstairs room. Suddenly, Jesus was in the room with them! They were afraid. They thought they were seeing a ghost. Jesus wanted them to know that it was really him and that he was really alive. So he let them touch him. And he asked for some food. When he ate a piece of fish, they knew he was alive!

How did Jesus let his helpers know he was alive?

DEAR JESUS, thank you for showing your helpers that you really were alive. Amen.

March 25

Thomas Believes

*Jesus told [Thomas],
"You believe because
you see me. Those who
believe without seeing
me will be truly happy."*
JOHN 20:29

Did you ever hear some news that was hard to believe? Maybe you said, "I'll believe it if I see it with my own eyes." Well, that's how it was with Thomas, one of Jesus' helpers. When his friends told him they had seen Jesus, he didn't believe them. A week later, Thomas saw Jesus and touched him. Then he believed. But Jesus wants all of us to believe that he is alive.

Can you see Jesus? Can you still believe that he is alive?

DEAR GOD, I can listen to Bible stories about your Son, Jesus, but I can't see him. Thank you for helping me to know that he is alive. Amen.

March 26

Saying Good-Bye

You must tell people to change their hearts and lives. If they do this, their sins will be forgiven.
LUKE 24:47

Sometimes when people go away, they give us jobs to do. Jesus knew he was soon going back home to his Father in heaven. So he gave his helpers a big job to do. He told them to teach people how to love and obey him. He told them to start right where they were, in their own city, and then to go everywhere. He said that God would help them.

What job did Jesus give his helpers? Can you be his helper too?

DEAR GOD, please be with all of the people who teach others about you. Amen.

March 27

Going Home

*Jesus rose into the sky. He went
up into a cloud.* ACTS 1:9

Jesus' work on earth was done, and it was time for
him to go home to heaven. He had lived there with
God the Father since way back at the beginning. Jesus
went up into the sky and disappeared. There was no
airplane—he just went up all by himself. Only God's Son,
Jesus, could do that. Two angels told his helpers that he would
come back again in the same way.

Where is your home? Where is Jesus' home?

DEAR GOD, thank you for letting your Son, Jesus, live on earth for a
while. I know he lives with you now, but I'm glad that he will come
back again someday. In Jesus' name. Amen.

March 28

A Place in Heaven

Jesus said, ". . . Trust in God. And trust in me. There are many rooms in my Father's house. . . . I am going there to prepare a place for you." JOHN 14:1-2

Before Jesus went back to heaven, he talked to his helpers about it. He told them what a big, wonderful place it was. He told them that when he went there, he would get a place ready for them, too! Then he would come back and take them to live with him. That promise is for everyone who loves him and trusts in him.

What is Jesus doing right now?

DEAR JESUS, thank you for wanting me to live with you someday. Thank you for getting a place ready for everyone who trusts in you. Amen.

thank you, Jesus

thank you for heaven

March 29

Coming Back

Look, Jesus is coming with the clouds!
Everyone will see him.
REVELATION 1:7

When you look up into the sky, what do you see? Do you see airplanes and birds and clouds? Of course you do! Do you see people? Of course not! People can't fly because they don't have wings, do they? But Jesus is special. When he went back to heaven, he went up into the sky. And when he comes back to earth, he will come down from the sky. Everyone will see him in the clouds!

How will Jesus come back to earth?

DEAR GOD, I'm glad your Son, Jesus, is coming back someday. I can't wait to see him! In Jesus' name. Amen.

March 30

No More Tears

He will wipe away every tear from their eyes. There will be no more death, sadness, crying, or pain.
REVELATION 21:4

Did you ever feel like crying? Maybe someone was unkind to you. Or your stomach hurt. Or you felt all alone. We all feel sad sometimes. But we won't feel that way in heaven! Everyone will be happy in heaven. No one will get hurt or feel sad. There will be a lot of singing but no crying. God will wipe away all of our tears! Everyone who loves God's Son, Jesus, will live with him there forever.

What will be special about living in heaven?

DEAR GOD, heaven sounds like a wonderful place. I can sing and be happy there forever. Thank you! Amen.

March 31

I'll See You Soon!

Jesus is the One who says that these things are true. Now he says, "Yes, I am coming soon." Amen. Come, Lord Jesus!
REVELATION 22:20

When someone we love goes away, we feel sad. We want that person to come back again. Well, at the end of the Bible, Jesus promised that he is coming back soon! We don't know how soon that will be. It might be today or tomorrow or someday when you're grown up or when you have children that are grown up! Whenever he comes back, you can give Jesus a big hug!

What special promise did Jesus make?

DEAR GOD, it will be a very special day when your Son, Jesus, comes back. I want to be ready to go and live with him in heaven. In Jesus' name. Amen.

April 1

A Perfect Father

Jesus said to them,
"When you pray, say:
'Father, we pray that your
name will always be kept
holy.'" LUKE 11:2

Fathers are usually pretty good about letting us talk to them whenever we want to. But sometimes they're busy or tired. God, our Father in heaven, is never tired and never too busy to listen.

Before Jesus went home to heaven, his friends asked him to teach them how to pray. Jesus said we could call God "Father." He said we should pray that God's name would always be thought of as perfect and holy. We should believe that God is good. He never does anything bad.

What can you call God when you pray?

DEAR FATHER IN HEAVEN, you are a perfect Father. You always love me and help me do what's right. Thank you! In Jesus' name. Amen.

April 2

Praying for Food

Give us our food day by day.
LUKE 11:3

When you're hungry, your mom or your dad probably gives you something to eat. So why do you need to ask God for food? Well, who helps your family earn money to buy food? God does! And who makes plants grow? God does! (A lot of your food comes from plants, you know.) God loves you and wants you to have everything you need. He just wants you to ask him for it!

What are some things you need each day? Who wants to help you have those things?

DEAR GOD, please give me plenty of food to eat today. Thank you for giving me everything I need. In Jesus' name. Amen.

April 3

I'm Sorry

Forgive our sins. LUKE 11:4

Did you ever make anyone feel like crying? Sometimes accidents happen. We do something that turns out bad, but we didn't mean to do it. Other times we do bad things on purpose. We do things that God doesn't want us to do. These bad things that we do on purpose are called "sins."

Our sins make everyone sad. But we can do something about that! We can tell God we're sorry, and he will forgive us. He will also help us tell the people we've hurt that we're sorry.

Who will forgive you for the bad things you have done?

DEAR GOD, when I do bad things, help me remember to tell you that I'm sorry. I know you'll forgive me. And you'll help me to be kind. In Jesus' name. Amen.

April 4

Forgiving Friends

Forgive our sins. For we have forgiven those who sinned against us. LUKE 11:4

Did anyone ever make you feel like crying? Sometimes your friends do bad things just like you do. Maybe a friend made you feel angry and you wanted to do something unkind back to your friend.

But what do you think God wants you to do? He wants you to forgive your friend just as he forgives you! Loving your friends and giving them hugs is better than being angry, isn't it?

If someone tells you, "I'm sorry," what should you do?

DEAR GOD, I want to be like you. I want to forgive my friends just as you forgive me. In Jesus' name. Amen.

April 5

Don't Tempt Me!

Don't allow us to be tempted.
LUKE 11:4

There it is—right on the shelf above you—a jar of your favorite candy! Your family has a rule that says, "No candy before dinner." But no one is around just now. So you're tempted to take a piece.

Jesus says we should pray that we won't be tempted to do things that are wrong. Not obeying our family's rules is wrong, isn't it?

God is always with us, ready to help when we feel like doing something that's wrong.

Did anyone ever tempt you to do something bad? Were you ever tempted because you thought no one would know?

DEAR GOD, thanks for letting me talk to you when I'm tempted to do something bad. I want to obey you and not give in to the wrong things that tempt me. In Jesus' name. Amen.

April 6

Pray and Sing Praises

If one of you is having troubles, he should pray.
If one of you is happy, he should sing praises.
JAMES 5:13

Think about a time when you were having trouble.
Maybe you got hurt or broke a favorite toy.
Did you pray about it? You should have. The Bible
tells you so!

Think about a time when you were very
happy. Maybe you visited Grandpa and
Grandma or got a new puppy or had fun at a
party. Did you tell God about it and sing him
a happy song of praise? You should have. The Bible tells you so!

When should you talk to God? When should you sing praises to him?

DEAR GOD, I'm so glad I can tell you everything. I can talk to you when
I'm sad, and I can sing praises to you when I'm happy. I love you, God.
Amen.

April 7

Anytime, Anyplace

Never stop praying.
1 THESSALONIANS 5:17

We can talk to God in the sunshine. Should we stop when the sun disappears? No! We should "never stop praying." We can talk to God when the rain pours down and we see a rainbow. Should we stop when the rainbow disappears? No! We should "_____." We can talk to God by a tree or by the ocean. Should we stop when we go inside? No! We should "_____."

Is there ever a time when you should stop praying?

DEAR GOD, thank you for wanting me to talk to you all the time. Thank you for always listening to my prayers. In Jesus' name. Amen.

April 8

The Best Answer

You will call to the Lord, and the Lord will answer you. ISAIAH 58:9

A little boy once wanted some berries that his mother knew would not be good to eat. They could make him sick, so she said no. She knew what was best.

God knows even more than mothers do! He always knows just how to answer our prayers. We might call to God and say, "Lord, please give me this. And give me that." God might say yes. He might say no. Or he might just tell us to wait.

Why does God sometimes say no or make us wait?

DEAR GOD, thank you for helping my family know what's best for me. And thank you for knowing the very best way to answer my prayers. Amen.

April 9

How to Live

All Scripture is given by God and is useful for teaching and for showing people what is wrong in their lives. 2 TIMOTHY 3:16

If your mom's washing machine doesn't work, she'll have to figure out what's wrong with it. She'll need an instruction book, won't she? She'll need a book that was written by the people who made the washing machine.

God wrote an instruction book too. It's called the Bible. God's words in the Bible help people know when they're doing things that are wrong. God knows just what to tell us because he made us!

How does God help us know what's right and what's wrong?

DEAR GOD, thank you for making me and for helping me know how I should live. Amen.

April 10

Paying Attention

The Lord . . . said, "Samuel, Samuel!"
Samuel said, "Speak, Lord. I am . . .
listening." I SAMUEL 3:10

Did anyone ever try to talk to you, but you didn't hear the person because you weren't paying attention?

Samuel heard a voice. He was paying attention, but he didn't know who was calling. Then he found out it was God! So he told God that he was listening.

We don't usually hear God's voice today. But God wants us to pay attention when someone reads Bible stories. Then we'll learn what God wants us to know.

How can you learn what God wants you to know?

DEAR GOD, I like to listen to Bible stories. Help me to always pay attention so I can learn all about you. In Jesus' name. Amen.

April 11

Help Me Understand!

*Jesus' followers asked him,
"What does this story mean?"*
LUKE 8:9

Maybe your mom looked in an instruction book to find out how to fix her washing machine, but she couldn't figure it out. So she called the store where she bought it and asked them to help her understand the instructions. Then she could make her washing machine work.

Sometimes we need help to understand God's instructions in the Bible, too. We can do the same thing that Jesus' Bible-time followers did. We can ask him to help us understand what our Bible stories mean.

Who can help you understand God's instructions?

DEAR JESUS, I want to understand everything in the Bible. Thank you for helping me. Amen.

April 12

"I'll Show You"

When Jesus was leaving, he saw a man named Matthew. . . . Jesus said to him, "Follow me."
MATTHEW 9:9

In the pictures, a teacher is showing a girl how to draw flowers. And she is showing a boy how to put his train tracks together.

Jesus asked people to follow him around so he could show them something too. He showed them how to be kind, how to love each other, and how to love God, his heavenly Father. He'll show us, too, if we listen to Bible stories and talk to him.

What does Jesus want to show us?

DEAR JESUS, you can show me lots of things. I pray that you'll show me how you want me to act every day. Amen.

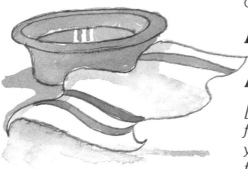

April 13

A Good Example

[Jesus said,] "I . . . have washed your feet. . . . I did this as an example for you. So you should do as I have done for you." JOHN 13:14-15

Do you get tired of picking up your toys? Does your mom ask you to do other things you wish you didn't have to do?

In Bible times, people wore sandals and walked on dusty roads, so their feet got hot and dirty. But no one liked to wash another person's feet. Jesus washed his helpers' feet. He did it as an example for them to follow. He wants people to help each other, even when it isn't fun.

How can you follow Jesus' example?

DEAR GOD, thank you for sending Jesus to be a good example. Help me to be like him. Amen.

April 14

God Is Real!

[God] did things to prove he is real:
He . . . gives you rain from heaven and crops
at the right times. He gives you food and fills
your hearts with joy. ACTS 14:17

You can't see God, can you? But does that mean he isn't real? Of course not! You can know that God is real by the wonderful things he does. He sends sunshine and clouds and rain. He makes crops grow in the fields so we can have food to eat. He even gives us fish and kittens to take care of!

What things does God give you to make you happy?

DEAR GOD, I can't see you, but I can see what you have made. And I can enjoy everything you give me. Thanks, God! Amen.

April 15

God's Flowers

Look at the flowers in the field. . . . I tell you that even Solomon with his riches was not dressed as beautifully as one of these flowers. MATTHEW 6:28-29

Jesus said we can learn about God by looking at the flowers he made. Flowers are so beautiful, it's as if they are wearing colorful clothes. Solomon was a rich king, but his clothes weren't as beautiful as flowers.

God wants you to let him take care of you just the way he takes care of the flowers!

Which of God's flowers do you like best?

DEAR GOD, thank you for taking care of your flowers—and me! Amen.

April 16

God Is Kind to Everyone

Your Father causes the sun to rise on good people and on bad people. Your Father sends rain to those who do good and to those who do wrong. MATTHEW 5:45

God is our special Father in heaven. He knows that some people do good things that are right to do. Others do bad things that are wrong to do. But God loves everyone. So he doesn't keep the sun from shining on the bad people. And he doesn't keep the rain away from the good people.

Was anyone ever mean to you? How will you treat that person if you try to be like God?

DEAR GOD, it's hard to love some people, but you do it. Help me to do it too. Amen.

April 17

Obeying Is Wise

[Jesus said,] "All who listen to my teachings and follow them are wise. They are like a man who builds his house on solid rock." MATTHEW 7:24

Do you build houses from blocks? Do you build houses in the sand? How long do your houses last?

The house you live in will last a long time. But it wouldn't last if it were built in the sand, would it?

Jesus said that a wise person builds a house on solid ground, with hard rock under it. Then wind and rainstorms can't knock it over. Jesus also said that a wise person listens to him and obeys him.

Who is it that you should obey if you want to be wise?

DEAR JESUS, thank you for keeping me safe when I'm wise enough to obey you. Amen.

April 18

Love Like Jesus

[Jesus said,] "Love each other. You must love each other as I have loved you." JOHN 13:34

We can say that we love someone, but it's not enough just to say it. We need to do something about it! We need to show our love by the way we act and by the things we do. That's what Jesus did. He showed his love for people by being kind to them and by helping them.

What are some kind things you can do for the people you love?

DEAR JESUS, thank you for loving me. Thank you for showing your love by listening to my prayers and helping me every day. Show me how to help the people I love. Amen.

April 19

Get Rid of the Garbage!

Stop lying to each other. Tell the truth.
EPHESIANS 4:25

If your friend says that you kicked him but you didn't, you feel bad, don't you?

If you get the carpet dirty but you tell Mom it was your brother, he might get in trouble. When your mom finds out it was you, she'll be upset. The next time you tell her something, she may not believe you.

God says that we should tell the truth. So we can't tell lies to each other if we want to obey God. Lies are like garbage—we want to get rid of them!

Why is it wrong to tell a lie?

DEAR GOD, I'm sorry about any lies I've told. I want to obey you, so please help me to always tell the truth. In Jesus' name. Amen.

April 20

Being Kind

Be kind and loving to each other.
EPHESIANS 4:32

It may seem easy to be kind to someone who feels good and can do kind things for you, too. But when someone is sick in bed, should you be kind anyway? Sure! Maybe you can share your favorite stuffed animal.

Some of your friends may not be able to do all of the things you can do. So you can be helpful. That's the loving thing to do.

What's one way that you can be kind and loving?

DEAR GOD, I want to make you happy by doing kind, loving things for my family and friends. Amen.

April 21

Happy to Do It

God loves the person who gives happily.
2 CORINTHIANS 9:7

Some Bible people had a lot of money. They had more than they needed. Other Bible people didn't have enough money to buy food or clothes.
The people who had more than they needed shared their money. Many of them were happy to give what they could.

God wants us to be happy to give what we can. If we don't have money to give, we can give our help.

How does God want us to feel about giving our money and our help to others?

DEAR GOD, I'm sorry about the times when I've grumbled about having to give my money or my help. Help me to be happy about doing it next time. In Jesus' name. Amen.

April 22

A Big Help

The baby's sister stood a short distance away. She wanted to see what would happen to him.
EXODUS 2:4

Mother hid Miriam's baby brother in the tall grass by the river. She did it so he would be safe from the mean king. Miriam wanted to be sure that her baby brother stayed safe. So she watched the baby until the king's daughter found him. This princess named the baby Moses. She let Miriam get someone to care for him. So Miriam got her mother! Miriam was a very good helper.

What can you do to be a good helper?

DEAR GOD, I want to be a big help to my family. Show me how to be a good helper tomorrow. Amen.

April 23

Helping Sick People

His skin became as healthy as a little child's! He was healed!
2 KINGS 5:14

General Naaman was an important man, but he had bad sores on his skin. Nothing would take them away. Naaman's wife had a helper. This girl told Naaman's wife about Elisha. The girl said that Elisha was a man who loved God, and he could help Naaman get rid of the sores. Elisha did help. He had the general wash in a river seven times. Naaman not only got well but he learned to love God too!

In what two ways did a little girl help Naaman?

DEAR GOD, please show me how to help sick people feel better. But most of all, show me how to help them love *you!* Amen.

DON'T JUST SIT THERE!

April 24

Obeying Parents

Children, obey your parents in all things. This pleases the Lord.
COLOSSIANS 3:20

Did you know that God planned for your parents to love you and care for you? He wants you to show your love for them by obeying them. God is pleased when you do that! God planned for you to learn many things from your parents too. They know what is best for you—like when it's time to go to bed or when it's safe to cross the street.

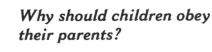

Why should children obey their parents?

DEAR LORD, thank you for the way my mom and dad love me and care for me. Help me to please you by obeying them. Amen.

April 25

Always Thankful

No matter what happens, always be thankful. I THESSALONIANS 5:18

When you're happy and having fun, it's easy to find things to thank God for, isn't it? But what about times when you get hurt or feel sad? What about rainy days when you want to play outside? Even during those times, you can find something to thank God for. You can be thankful that God loves you and understands how you feel—because he does, you know!

When should you be thankful?

DEAR GOD, thank you for happy times. Thank you for being with me and helping me when I'm hurt or sad, too. Amen.

WITH THANKS

April 26

Only One Thank-You

One . . . came back to Jesus. . . . He thanked Jesus for what he had done. LUKE 17:15-16

One time Jesus made ten men well. But nine of them hurried away. Only one man said thank you.

Sometimes we pray, "Jesus, please help me to feel better." Or we ask Jesus to take away Mom's headache. Or we ask him to help a friend. But when Jesus answers, we don't say thank you.

Jesus feels sad when we forget about him.

What should you say when Jesus helps you?

DEAR JESUS, thank you for the many ways that you help me every day. Amen.

April 27

Thanks for the Food

Look! I have given you all the plants and all the fruit trees for your food. GENESIS 1:29

Bible people grew fruit trees and had vegetable gardens. They baked round loaves of bread from grain that grew in farmers' fields. And they thanked God for their food.

Where do you get your food? No matter where you get it, God is the one who made the plants and trees that much of your food comes from. He is happy when you thank him before you eat.

What foods are you most thankful for?

DEAR GOD, you are good, you are great, and I thank you for my food! Amen.

April 28

The Winners

*How we thank
God . . . !
He makes us
the winners
because of
Jesus Christ
our Lord!*
1 CORINTHIANS
15:57

Baby Jesus grew up and taught people how to live for God. Then he died and came back to life. Now he wants to be our Lord. He wants to be in charge of our lives so we can be winners. Even if we feel left out like the girl in the picture, we can be winners. Everyone who loves Jesus will live with him in heaven someday. That's a winning prize to thank God for!

How can Jesus help you to be a winner?

DEAR GOD, thank you for your Son, Jesus. I want him to be my Lord and to be in charge of me. Then I'll be a winner and live in heaven forever! Amen.

April 29

Thank-You Songs

Make music to the Lord . . .
with harps and the sound of
singing. Blow the trumpets. . . .
Shout for joy to the Lord.
PSALM 98:5-6

Bible people often sang thank-you songs to God. And they played musical instruments, like harps and horns.

We can sing to God too. We can play harps, guitars, and pianos. We can blow horns and beat drums. We should do these things to praise God for being who he is—a great God who loves us very much.

Can you sing today's prayer to the tune of "Jesus Loves Me" or beat your drum as you say it?

DEAR GOD, I thank you.
Dear God, I thank you.
Dear God, I thank you for
loving me each day. Amen.

April 30

Thanks for Jesus!

*Thank God for his Son—his Gift
too wonderful for words.*
2 CORINTHIANS 9:15

Did you ever get a gift that was so special you didn't know what to say? You were so excited that all you could do was jump up and down, clap your hands, and give a big hug to the person who gave the gift!

When we think about how God sent us his Son, Jesus, we should feel the same way. We can show our thanks with a loud shout or a quiet prayer that's like a hug for God.

Who sent Jesus to this world as a gift to each of us?

DEAR GOD, thank you for letting your Son come to this earth for a while. I love him very much. Amen.

May 1

The Garden of Eden

The Lord God planted a garden in the East, in a place called Eden.
GENESIS 2:8

Way back in the beginning, long before Jesus came to live on this earth, God made a Garden. It was a beautiful place, with grass and flowers and trees. Wild animals were everywhere! God made the Garden of Eden for the first people, Adam and Eve. He wanted this Garden to be their home. He even let Adam name the animals.

Why did God make a beautiful Garden?

DEAR GOD, thank you for green grass, pretty flowers, and big trees. Thanks for all the animals, too! Amen.

May 2

What God Said

You must not eat the fruit from the tree which gives the knowledge of good and evil. GENESIS 2:17

God told Adam it would be OK to eat fruit from the trees in the Garden. But there was one tree in the middle of the Garden that no one was to eat from. The fruit from that tree would teach people about evil or bad things. If they didn't eat that fruit, people would never have to know about anything bad. God gave people a choice. They could obey him or disobey him. We have that choice too.

What did God tell Adam not to do?

DEAR GOD, help me to choose to obey you. In Jesus' name. Amen.

May 3

Satan Talks to Eve

The snake said to the woman, ". . . God knows that if you eat the fruit from that tree, you will learn about good and evil. Then you will be like God!" GENESIS 3:4-5

A snake talked to Eve in the beautiful Garden. The snake made it sound as if doing what was wrong would be OK. Eve began to think that disobeying God might be fun. She didn't know that the snake was really Satan. Satan is another name for the devil, and he hates God. So he was trying to make her do something bad.

What did Satan want Eve to do?

DEAR GOD, help me not to listen when someone tries to make me do something bad. In Jesus' name. Amen.

May 4

The Wrong Choice

The woman saw that the tree was beautiful. . . . So she took some of its fruit and ate it. She also gave some of the fruit to her husband, and he ate it. GENESIS 3:6

Eve believed Satan, who had told her it would be OK to eat the fruit she wanted. Eve ate the fruit, and so did Adam. Satan got his way. He wanted people to do bad things and get in trouble. God felt sad. He had told Adam and Eve how to obey him, but they didn't listen.

Did Adam and Eve listen to God or to Satan?

DEAR GOD, I know you love me and want what is best for me. Help me to listen to what you say in the Bible. In Jesus' name. Amen.

May 5

Hiding from God

The man and his wife hid from the Lord God among the trees in the garden. GENESIS 3:8

When God made Adam and Eve, they knew only about good things. But then they ate the fruit God had said not to eat. And it was just the way God had said it would be. Now they knew about bad things. And when they heard God walking in the Garden, they hid among the trees.

Were Adam and Eve happy to see God after they disobeyed him?

DEAR GOD, when I do wrong things, help me not to run away from you. Help me to talk to you and tell you I'm sorry. Amen.

May 6

"Don't Blame Me!"

*The man said, "You gave this woman to me.
She gave me fruit from the tree. So I ate it."
Then . . . the woman . . . answered,
"The snake tricked me."* GENESIS 3:12-13

Did you ever get caught doing something you knew you shouldn't have been doing? Maybe you said your sister or brother made you do it. Or maybe you said the other kids you were playing with started it. Does that sound a little like what Adam and Eve said to God?

The next time you do something that's wrong, don't blame someone else!

Who did Adam blame for what he did wrong? Who did Eve blame?

DEAR GOD, when I do something I shouldn't do, help me not to blame other people. Amen.

May 7

Trouble Comes

God said to the woman, "I will cause you to have much trouble. . . ." God said to the man, "You . . . will have to work very hard for food. . . . The ground will produce thorns and weeds for you."
GENESIS 3:16-18

God wanted Adam and Eve to obey him and be happy. He wanted to let them live forever in the Garden with no problems. But they didn't obey. So God sent trouble into the world. But he also made plans to send his Son, Jesus, into the world. Jesus would help people obey God.

Why did God send trouble into the world?

DEAR GOD, thank you for your Son, Jesus, who helps me obey you. Amen.

May 8

Everyone Is a Sinner, But . . .

Adam caused many to be sinners because he disobeyed God. Christ caused many to be welcome to God because he obeyed. ROMANS 5:19

Adam, who was the very first person, didn't obey God. He sinned, so he was called a sinner. Because of what he did, everyone is a sinner. But think about how different Jesus is from Adam! Jesus Christ never sinned. Because he obeyed his heavenly Father and died on the cross for us, we're all welcome to join God's family. If we trust Jesus, God won't even think of us as sinners.

Why should we trust Jesus?

DEAR GOD, thank you for Jesus, who never sinned. Thank you that I can trust him and be in your family. In Jesus' name. Amen.

May 9

Clothes for Adam and Eve

The Lord God made clothes from animal skins for the man and his wife.
GENESIS 3:21

It would be a long time before God sent his Son, Jesus, into the world. Right now, God had to take care of Adam and Eve. They were still the only people, and they had sinned. Did that mean God didn't love them anymore? No, God loved them very much. Because he loved them, he wanted them to have the things they needed. So he made clothes for them.

What kind thing did God do for Adam and Eve?

DEAR GOD, thank you for loving me and doing kind things for me even when I do things that are wrong. Amen.

May 10

Time to Leave

God said, "Look, the man . . . knows good and evil. And now we must keep him from eating some of the fruit from the tree of life."
GENESIS 3:22

There were two trees in the middle of the Garden. God had told Adam and Eve not to eat the fruit on one of them. But they did it anyway, so they learned about good and evil. The other tree was called the "tree of life." Now God wouldn't let Adam and Eve eat from this tree either. Because they hadn't obeyed, they couldn't stay in the Garden and live there forever.

Why couldn't Adam and Eve eat from the tree of life?

DEAR GOD, Adam and Eve must have made you feel very sad. Help me not to make you sad. Amen.

May 11

The Hard Work Begins

The Lord God sent [Adam] away from the Garden of Eden forever. He sent him out to farm the ground.
GENESIS 3:23

Life had been wonderful for Adam and Eve in the Garden. They didn't have to work, and there was plenty to eat. The animals were a lot of fun, and the flowers were pretty. But now they couldn't live there anymore. They had to work hard and grow their own food. They got very tired after working all day long.

How was life different outside the Garden?

DEAR GOD, show me how to help Mom and Dad with the hard work they have to do. Amen.

May 12

Angels Guard the Garden

God placed mighty angels at the east of the Garden of Eden.
They stood with a flaming sword to guard the entrance. GENESIS 3:24

Adam and Eve were never able to go back to the Garden. It was a perfect place, and people were not perfect anymore. They had sinned. Many years later, Jesus came to take away sin. People still cannot live forever in the Garden. But now we can go to heaven and live forever there!

Where can we live forever?

DEAR GOD, thank you that I can live forever in heaven, all because of your Son, Jesus. Amen.

May 13

The First Babies

Eve . . . gave birth to Cain. . . . After that, Eve gave birth to Cain's brother Abel.
GENESIS 4:1-2

Adam and Eve were the only people in the world. But God wanted his world to be filled with people. So God helped people to have babies. The very first baby to be born was a baby boy named Cain. Then Abel was born. Giving birth to babies was hard work for Eve, but it was worth it! She and Adam loved their babies. God loved them too.

What were the names of the first two babies?

DEAR GOD, thank you for babies! Thank you for loving me when I was a baby and for still loving me. I love you, too. Amen.

May 14

Growing and Learning

Stop doing wrong! Learn to do good.
ISAIAH 1:16-17

B abies don't know that there is a difference between right and wrong. When you were a baby, you just thought about yourself. If someone got in your way, you kicked and screamed. That's what all babies do. But then you started growing and learning. You found out that when you did bad things, you felt sad, and so did everyone else. But when you did good things, you felt happy. Others did too. Now you think about your friends. You want to do good things that make them happy.

What good things can you do to make your friends happy?

DEAR GOD, thank you for helping me to grow and learn to do good things.
Amen.

May 15

I Have Enough, Thank You!

Be satisfied with what you have. God has said, "I will never leave you." HEBREWS 13:5

Sometimes we want more and more things. Maybe we have a kitten, but a friend has a puppy. So we say, "I want one of those, too." Maybe we have a peanut-butter sandwich, but someone else has another kind. So we say, "I want one of those, too." God wants us to be satisfied to know that he is always with us. He gives us what we need so we can say, "I have enough, thank you!"

Name some things you have that God wants you to be satisfied with.

DEAR GOD, thank you for the good things you give me. Thank you most of all for always being with me. Amen.

May 16

Asking for Good Gifts

Your heavenly Father will give good things to those who ask him.
MATTHEW 7:11

If you asked God for a motorbike, he would probably say no. He wouldn't want you to get hurt. But if you told God you'd like a hug from the older woman next door, he might say yes.

We can't know for sure how God will answer our prayers. But we do know that he wants to give us good things. So those are the things we should ask for.

Why doesn't God give you everything you ask him for?

DEAR GOD, I'm glad I can ask you for things. I'll try to just ask for good things. In Jesus' name. Amen.

May 17

Doing Good and Being Happy

If a person pleases God, God will give him wisdom, knowledge and joy. ECCLESIASTES 2:26

God is pleased when we learn about him. Older people who love God like to help us do that. They can help us understand God's Word, the Bible. Knowing what God tells us in the Bible makes us wise. And when we do the good things that God tells us to do, we feel happy. We're filled with joy.

What can you do to become wise?

DEAR GOD, thank you for Sunday school teachers. I'm glad that my teacher helps me to learn what the Bible says about pleasing you. Amen.

May 18

Don't Act Important

It is wise not to be proud.
PROVERBS 11:2

Some people think they are better than anyone else. One person might think no one can climb a tree as well as she can. Another person might think he is the smartest person in the world. Someone else might think she is the prettiest person in her class. People like that are proud. They act as if they're more important than anyone else. But they aren't. God says, "It is wise not to be proud."

How does a proud person act?

DEAR GOD, help me not to be proud. Amen.

May 19

Watch What You Eat!

It is not good to eat too much honey. PROVERBS 25:27

Parties can be fun. There are balloons and games and kids. And there is so much food—cookies and cake and candy and lemonade. It's easy to eat too many sweets at a party. But the Bible says it's not good to eat too many sweet things. Even if your friends are eating too much, you can be wise. You can stop stuffing yourself so you don't get sick.

Why shouldn't you eat too many sweet things?

DEAR GOD, thank you for cookies and cake and candy. Help me to enjoy those sweets without eating too much of them. Amen.

May 20

Good Rules

Be sure to do everything I have commanded you.
DEUTERONOMY 12:32

Grown-ups have to learn rules for driving. They need to know when to stop and when to go so their cars won't all run into each other!

God has given us rules too. His rules say to worship him and to love each other. We're not to steal or lie or hurt anyone. God loves us so much that he commands us to obey his rules. That means we must do what he says. Then we'll be safe and happy.

Why is it good to do what God says?

DEAR GOD, help me to obey your rules so I'll be safe and happy. Amen.

TURN LEFT

TURN RIGHT

GO

STOP

SLOW

May 21

Take Away the Big Grasshoppers!

I will give my Spirit freely to all kinds of people.
Then anyone who asks the Lord for help will be saved.
JOEL 2:28, 32

Long before Jesus was born, something terrible happened to God's people. Big grasshoppers called locusts ate their trees and bushes and crops. But God promised that someday their troubles would end. He would send his Spirit. Then all people could ask for God's help. And he would save them from even bigger troubles!

Now God's promise has come true. He has sent his Spirit. So who can ask for God's help?

DEAR GOD, thank you for promising to send your Spirit and for keeping your promise. Amen.

May 22

Like the Wind

[Jesus said,] "You hear the wind blow. But you don't know where the wind comes from or where it is going. It is the same with every person who is born from the Spirit. JOHN 3:8

You can't see the wind. But you can feel it blowing on your face. And you can see what the wind does. The grass and flowers and trees bend in the wind. Jesus said that's how it is with the Holy Spirit. You can't see him, but you can feel his love. And you can see what he does when you let him help you do what's right.

How is the Holy Spirit like the wind?

DEAR GOD, I know that you are God the Father and that Jesus is God the Son. Now I'm glad to learn about God the Holy Spirit. Amen.

May 23

Jesus Did Good Things

You know about Jesus from Nazareth. God . . . [gave] him the Holy Spirit and power. You know how Jesus went everywhere doing good. ACTS 10:38

When Jesus lived on this earth, he did many good things. He helped sick people get well. He taught people about God, his Father in heaven. And he showed his love to everyone—little babies, children like you, and grown-ups like your mom and dad. The Holy Spirit helped Jesus do these good things. Now God wants to give the Holy Spirit to all of us.

What did the Holy Spirit help Jesus do?

DEAR GOD, thank you for the good things Jesus did when he lived on earth. Thank you for the Holy Spirit, who can help me do good things too. In Jesus' name. Amen.

May 24

Our Special Helper

[Jesus said,] "If I do not go away, then the Helper will not come." JOHN 16:7

Another name for the Holy Spirit is "Helper." When Jesus lived on earth, he was a person just like you and me. He could be in only one place at a time, just like you and me. So Jesus said it would be better for him to go back to heaven and send the Holy Spirit. And that's what he did! Now everyone who loves God can have the Holy Spirit's help at the same time.

Jesus' friends didn't want him to go away. Can you name the Helper Jesus promised to send in his place?

DEAR GOD, I love your Son, Jesus. And I'm glad he sent the Holy Spirit to be my special Helper. Amen.

May 25

What's True?

When the Spirit of truth comes he will lead you into all truth. JOHN 16:13

Jesus told his friends all about the Holy Spirit. He said that this special Spirit of God knows what is true and can help people understand the truth.

There are a lot of books to read. Some are just for fun—you know the stories aren't really true. But the Bible is filled with true stories. You can ask the Holy Spirit to help you understand what God wants you to learn from each story.

If you want to know the truth, who has the answer?

DEAR GOD, sometimes I wonder what's true and what's not true. I'm glad the Holy Spirit can help me figure it all out. Amen.

May 26

Waiting . . .

[Jesus told his friends] not to leave Jerusalem. He told them to wait there until the Holy Spirit came upon them. ACTS 1:4

Waiting can be hard, can't it? It's especially hard to wait for something you really want, like a visit from a friend. You wait and wait for your friend to come over so you can play. Your friend was supposed to come right after lunch. Well, you ate lunch, but your friend hasn't come yet. Your mom says to be patient and stay right by the house—your friend will come soon.

That's how it was when Jesus' friends waited for the Holy Spirit. Jesus told them to stay right in their city and wait. So they did.

Why did Jesus want his friends to stay in Jerusalem?

DEAR GOD, teach me to be patient when I need to wait. Help me to wait patiently for you to answer my prayers. In Jesus' name. Amen.

May 27

No More Waiting!

Suddenly a noise came from heaven. It sounded like a strong wind blowing. This noise filled the whole house where they were sitting.
ACTS 2:2

For ten days Jesus' friends had been waiting for the Holy Spirit. They were sitting quietly in a room on Sunday morning. All of a sudden, it wasn't quiet anymore! It sounded as if the wind were blowing hard. The noise was so loud it could be heard through the whole house. That's when the Holy Spirit came.

Who was waiting for the Holy Spirit?

DEAR GOD, I'm glad the Bible tells about the exciting time when the Holy Spirit came to Jesus' friends.
Amen.

May 28

The Holy Spirit Is Here

They saw something that looked like flames of fire. The flames were separated and stood over each person there. They were all filled with the Holy Spirit. ACTS 2:3-4

When the Holy Spirit first came to Jesus' friends, everyone could see a flame of fire over each of them. That was a special sign from God. People could see the fire on the outside. But what it really meant was that the Holy Spirit had come to live inside Jesus' friends.

Why were there flames of fire over Jesus' friends?

DEAR GOD, thank you for showing everyone that the Holy Spirit really came. Amen.

May 29

Everyone Can Understand

We are from different places. But we hear these men telling in our own languages about the great things God has done! ACTS 2:8, 11

Many people had come to Jerusalem to worship God. They were from different countries and spoke different languages. So they couldn't understand each other's words.

But when the Holy Spirit came to Jesus' friends, he helped them talk so that everyone could understand! Then Jesus' friends could tell everyone about Jesus.

What did the Holy Spirit help Jesus' friends do?

DEAR GOD, thank you for wanting everyone to understand the words people say about you and your Son, Jesus. Amen.

May 30

What Should We Do?

Peter said to them, "Change your hearts and lives and be baptized . . .
in the name of Jesus Christ for the forgiveness of your sins.
And you will receive the gift of the Holy Spirit." ACTS 2:38

Peter told the people in Jerusalem that Jesus died and came back to life. He said that God the Father gave the Holy Spirit to Jesus the Son. And now Jesus was giving the Spirit to everyone who wanted to live for him. Peter told people to turn away from bad things and be baptized, asking Jesus to forgive their sins. Then they would get the gift of the Holy Spirit.

What must we do to receive the Holy Spirit?

DEAR GOD, thank you for the special gift of the Holy Spirit. Amen.

May 31

Power for You and Me

[Jesus said,] "The Holy Spirit will come to you. Then you will receive power. You will be my witnesses." ACTS 1:8

If a toy car needs a battery, it won't move without one, will it? The car needs the power that comes from a battery.

People who love Jesus need power too. We need the Holy Spirit to get us moving! He gives us the power to obey and be witnesses. Telling what they know is what witnesses do. We know a lot about Jesus, so the Holy Spirit can give us power to be Jesus' witnesses.

What kind of power does the Holy Spirit give us?

DEAR GOD, please give me power from the Holy Spirit to obey you and tell others about Jesus. Amen.

June 1

A Loving Shepherd

[Jesus said,] "Don't fear, little flock."
LUKE 12:32

Did you know that a group of sheep is called a "flock"? A flock of sheep follows its shepherd, and he makes sure that his sheep are safe. He loves his flock, especially the young lambs.

Jesus calls us his little flock. He wants us to know that we don't need to be afraid. He will take care of us and keep us safe.

Jesus is like a shepherd, and you're one of his little lambs. He loves you very much.

How is Jesus like a shepherd?

DEAR JESUS, you're my shepherd, and I'm one of your little lambs. So I don't have to be afraid. Thank you for loving me and keeping me safe. Amen.

June 2

No Time in Jail

We owed a debt because we broke God's laws. . . . But God forgave us that debt. He . . . nailed it to the cross.
COLOSSIANS 2:14

If people can't pay the money they owe someone, that money is called a "debt." Bible-time people were put in jail when they owed money. The Bible says that we owed a debt to God, but it wasn't money. It was the wrong things we did—we broke God's rules. But God sent Jesus to pay our debt. He died on a cross and came back to life. Now God forgives us—our debt is gone!

How did Jesus pay for the wrong things we've done?

DEAR JESUS, thank you for loving me so much that you paid the debt I owed God. Amen.

June 3

Gone Forever

You will throw away all our sins into the deepest sea. MICAH 7:19

Did you ever try to look down to the bottom of the ocean? An ocean, also called a "sea," is deeper than any swimming pool, pond, or lake. The deepest part of the sea is so deep that anything you'd put down there would be lost forever. The Bible says that when God forgives our sins, it's as if he throws them into the deepest sea. They are gone forever!

When God forgives our sins, what happens to them?

DEAR GOD, I'm glad you want to forgive my sins. I'm sorry for each one of them. In Jesus' name. Amen.

June 4

Wiped Away

[God said,] "I am the One who forgives all your sins. . . . I will not remember your sins." ISAIAH 43:25

When you wipe off a chalkboard, the words and pictures are gone, aren't they? Sometimes we do wrong things, like getting angry and knocking over a vase. Then we're sorry. We wish we could wipe away the wrong so it would seem as if we'd never done it. Well, that's just what God does! He forgives our sins and then forgets all about them.

When God forgives us, does he remember our sins?

DEAR GOD, please forgive me for the bad things I've done and forget I ever did them. Help me to forget too. In Jesus' name. Amen.

June 5

Everyone Needs Jesus

Everyone who believes in Jesus will be forgiven. God will forgive his sins through Jesus. ACTS 10:43

Some people are so nice. It seems that they never do anything bad. Maybe you have a friend like that. Perhaps that's what your grandma or your Sunday school teacher or your mom or your dad is like. But the Bible says that even nice people need to be forgiven. Everyone has done things that are wrong. Big people have, and little people have. So everyone needs Jesus. God will forgive everyone who believes that Jesus is his Son.

Who needs to be forgiven?

DEAR GOD, thank you for your promise to forgive everyone who believes in Jesus. Amen.

June 6

God Said It First

We love because God first loved us. I JOHN 4:19

Did your family love you when you were a baby? Of course they did! Your mom may have said to you, "I loved you even before you were born!" That's what God says too. He has always loved you, and he will keep on loving you after you grow up. Because God loves you, you want to love him back, don't you? His love for you helps you love other people, too!

What does God's love for you help you to do?

DEAR GOD, thank you for your love. I love you, too! And I love my family and my friends. Amen.

June 7

I Forgive You

Forgive each other just as God forgave you in Christ.
EPHESIANS 4:32

When you tell God you're sorry about doing something bad, does he need to think about whether or not he will forgive you? No! God will forgive you right away because of Jesus Christ.

What about you? When someone is sorry about hurting you or making you sad, do you have to think about whether or not to forgive that person? Or are you ready to give a hug and say, "I forgive you"?

What should you say when people tell you they're sorry?

DEAR GOD, I know you forgive me, and I thank you for that. Help me to forgive others even when I don't feel like it. In Jesus' name. Amen.

June 8

You Don't Have to Pay

The servant fell down before the king. . . . He said, "Oh, sir, be patient with me. I will find a way to pay. . . ." Then the king . . . let his servant go and said he didn't have to pay back his debt.
MATTHEW 18:26-27

Jesus told a story about a king. The king had a helper who owed him a lot of money. When the helper said he couldn't pay the money back right away, the king felt sorry for him. He said, "You don't have to pay back any of the money you owe me."

God is kind just like that king. He forgives us for our sins.

How was a king kind to his servant? How is God kind to you?

DEAR GOD, thank you for being kind like that king. In Jesus' name. Amen.

June 9

Pay Me!

That same servant found another servant who owed
him a few dollars. The servant . . . said, "Pay me the money
you owe me!" MATTHEW 18:28

Jesus told about a king who was kind. He had a helper who owed him a lot of money, but the king didn't make the man pay. But then what did the helper do? He found another man who owed him just a little money. He grabbed him and told him he had to pay. When the man couldn't pay, he threw the man into jail.

Was the king's helper kind?

DEAR GOD, you are so kind to me. Help me to be kind to my friends. In Jesus' name. Amen.

June 10

The King Is Upset

The man's friends went to the king. They told him what had happened. Then the angry king sent the man to prison.
MATTHEW 18:31, 34

J esus said that a king was kind and forgave his helper. But that helper was unkind to another man. He wouldn't forgive the man. Instead, he put him in jail. The man's friends told the king. Then the king became angry and sent his helper to jail. The king was fair, wasn't he? God is fair too.

Why did the king become angry with his helper?

DEAR GOD, you are a great king. I'm glad you are always fair. Amen.

June 11

Don't Refuse to Forgive

[The king said,] "I forgave you . . . just because you asked me to. Shouldn't you have had mercy on others, just as I had mercy on you?" MATTHEW 18:32-33

The king in Jesus' story had mercy on his helper. That means he felt sorry for his helper, so he was kind and loving to him. How was he kind? He forgave his helper just because the man asked him to. Jesus told this story so we would know how kind and loving God is. And he told it to show us that we should forgive others just because they ask us to.

When it's hard to forgive someone, how can Jesus' story help you?

DEAR GOD, help me to forgive others for the bad things they do just as you forgive me for the bad things I do. Amen.

June 12

Say It and Mean It!

Forgive your brother from your heart. MATTHEW 18:35

Did your big brother ever say something unkind and then tell you he was sorry? Did your dad ever break a promise to do something and then tell you he was sorry? Maybe you said, "Oh, that's all right." But you didn't really mean it. You still felt upset and acted angry.

Jesus doesn't want you to just say you forgive someone. He wants you to *mean* what you say.

What should you stop doing if you really forgive someone?

DEAR GOD, whenever I tell someone, "I forgive you," help me to mean the words I say. In Jesus' name. Amen.

June 13

Get Out of My Way!

If we confess our sins, [God] will forgive our sins.
1 JOHN 1:9

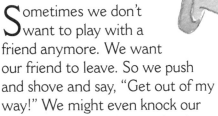

Sometimes we don't want to play with a friend anymore. We want our friend to leave. So we push and shove and say, "Get out of my way!" We might even knock our friend down. That's not a kind way to act, is it? Being unkind is wrong. It's a sin we need to confess to God. That means we need to tell him what we did and say we're sorry. Then he will forgive us and help us tell our friend we're sorry too.

What does it mean to confess your sins?

DEAR GOD, sometimes I'm not as kind as I should be. I'm sorry. Please forgive me and help me to do what's right. In Jesus' name. Amen.

June 14

When Can I Stop?

Peter . . . asked, "Lord, when my brother sins against me . . . must I . . . forgive him as many as 7 times?"
MATTHEW 18:21

P eter knew that people often do bad things over and over again. So he wondered how many times he had to forgive people like that. Maybe seven times? That would be every day for a week! Jesus surprised Peter by saying that seven times wasn't enough. Jesus gave him a really, really big number. That meant Jesus doesn't want people to ever stop forgiving each other.

Is it ever OK to stop forgiving someone?

DEAR GOD, I'm glad you never stop forgiving me. Help me to never stop forgiving others. Amen.

June 15

Four Friends

Some people came, bringing a paralyzed man to Jesus. Four of them were carrying the paralyzed man. MARK 2:3

A young man could not walk. He was paralyzed. His friends cared about him and wanted to help him. Well, they heard that Jesus was in town. So four of them laid their friend on a mat and carried him to the house where Jesus was. The men were excited. They were sure that Jesus would know what to do.

Why did some men take their friend to Jesus?

DEAR GOD, thank you for people who can walk and for people who can't. I know you love them all, and so do I! Amen.

June 16

A Good Idea

They could not get to Jesus because of the crowd. So they went to the roof above Jesus and made a hole in the roof. MARK 2:4

How could a hole in a roof be a good idea? One time it was! Four men were carrying their friend on a mat because he couldn't walk. They carried the man up an outside stairway, getting him to a flat roof. It was on the house where Jesus was. The roof was made of mud and sticks, so it was easy to make a hole. Jesus looked up to see what was going on and saw a man coming down through the roof!

What good idea did God give the four friends?

DEAR GOD, thank you for the good ideas you give us when we want to help our friends. In Jesus' name. Amen.

June 17

Jesus Helps

Jesus saw that these men had great faith. So he said to the paralyzed man, "Young man, your sins are forgiven."
MARK 2:5

The man on the mat couldn't walk. He needed Jesus' help. But first Jesus forgave his sins. Jesus saw that the man and his friends "had great faith." That means each one believed with all his heart that Jesus could help. So he did! After he forgave the man, he told him to stand up and walk.

What two things did Jesus do for the young man?

DEAR GOD, I'm glad I can pray for my friends. It's like bringing them to Jesus the way the four men brought their friend. Amen.

June 18

Paul Was Wrong

[Paul said,] "I used to believe that I should punish the followers of Jesus. I even chased them to distant cities." ACTS 26:9, 11

At one time Paul didn't think Jesus was God's Son. After Jesus went back to heaven, Paul began to hurt Jesus' followers. Paul thought he was doing the right thing, but he was wrong. He should have talked to the people he was hurting. They could have helped him know Jesus.

What did Paul do that was wrong?

DEAR GOD, help me to believe that Jesus is your Son. Help me to listen to my Sunday school teacher and others who love Jesus. Amen.

June 19

A Light from Heaven

One day . . . a light from Heaven shone down on me. . . . I heard a voice speaking to me. . . . The voice said, ". . . I am Jesus, the one you are trying to hurt." ACTS 26:13-15

Paul was going to a town far away. He wanted to hurt people there who loved Jesus. But while he was on the road, a very bright light began to shine on him. And Jesus talked to him from heaven! Jesus said that when Paul hurt people, he was hurting Jesus, too. Jesus wanted Paul to help people, not hurt them. It was time for Paul to teach people that Jesus really is God's Son.

What happened to Paul along a road one day?

DEAR JESUS, thank you for helping Paul learn to know you. Thank you for helping me to learn about you too. Amen.

June 20

Paul's New Job

*[Jesus said to Paul,] "I have chosen you to be . . . my witness.
I send you [so that people] may turn . . . to God. Then their sins
can be forgiven.* ACTS 26:16, 18

Before Jesus talked to Paul through a bright light, Paul did not believe in Jesus. He tried to get rid of people who did. After Jesus talked to him from heaven, Paul went everywhere to tell people about it. He walked to some places and went by boat to others. He told people to believe in Jesus. Then God would forgive their sins.

What did Paul tell people everywhere?

DEAR GOD, thank you for people who teach others about Jesus. I want to learn more about him so I can tell people what I know too. Amen.

June 21

Knock, Knock! Jesus Is There!

[Jesus said,] "I stand at the door and knock. If anyone hears my voice and opens the door, I will come in and eat with him."
REVELATION 3:20

It's fun when friends come to visit and eat with you, isn't it? Well, Jesus wants to be your very special friend. He's not living on earth right now—he's living in heaven. But he still wants to be part of your life. He wants to be with you all the time. He can be—all you have to do is invite him in!

Can you see Jesus? Can he still be your special friend?

DEAR JESUS, I love you, and I want you to be my friend. Please come and be with me all the time. Amen.

June 22

The Answer Will Come

Ask, and you will be given what you ask for. . . .
Everyone who asks, receives. MATTHEW 7:7-8

If you asked your mom for cake before dinner, do you think she would tell you to wait? She might say, "Ask me again after dinner." Sometimes we ask God for things that he is not ready to give us. He knows it's not the right time. Or maybe he has an even better gift for us! But God doesn't want us to give up. He wants us to keep asking, and he will give us just the right thing at just the right time.

What should we do when we want something from God?

DEAR GOD, thanks for letting me ask you for things. Thanks for knowing just how to answer my prayers. In Jesus' name. Amen.

June 23

God Keeps His Promises

When the right time came, God sent his Son. . . . His purpose was to make us his children. God will give you what he promised, because you are his child.
GALATIANS 4:4-5, 7

Your parents like to do things for you because you are their child and they love you. Well, God wants you to be a child in his family too. He sent Jesus so you can believe in him and join his family. God promises to love and forgive you. He will help you have what you need, and he also promises that he will never leave you!

What are some of God's promises to you?

DEAR GOD, I love my family. And I'm glad that I can be a child in your family too. In Jesus' name. Amen.

June 24

We Keep Pleasing Jesus

As you received Christ Jesus the Lord, so continue to live in him. COLOSSIANS 2:6

When you choose to be in God's family, you receive a gift. That gift is Jesus! He comes to live with you and help you.

Receiving Jesus is like having a birthday. But guess what sometimes happens to birthday gifts. We forget about them. That's not a good thing to do, is it? We don't want to forget about Jesus either. We want to keep pleasing him and letting him help us.

Since Jesus is our friend, what do we want to keep doing?

DEAR JESUS, thank you for wanting to live with me and help me. I don't ever want to forget about you. Amen.

June 25

And the Winner Is . . .

You know that in a race all the runners run. But only one gets the prize. So run like that. Run to win!
1 CORINTHIANS 9:24

Did you know that living for Jesus is like running in a race? When you're in a race, you must try to keep running until the end. You can't stop trying if you want to win. When you're living for Jesus, you must try to keep pleasing him until the end. You can't stop living for him now if you want to live with him in heaven someday.

How is living for Jesus like running in a race?

DEAR JESUS, I'm happy when I run, and I'm happy when I do my best to please you. I love you! Amen.

June 26

A Prize That Lasts

*All those who compete in the games
use strict training. They do this so that they can
win a crown . . . that lasts only a short time.
But our crown will continue forever.*
1 CORINTHIANS 9:25

Many people compete against each other in the Olympic Games. There are different sports, and everyone tries to win a gold medal. In Bible times, the winners in these games received a crown of leaves. But the green leaves would dry up and have to be thrown away. People who love Jesus will get a different kind of crown. We'll get a prize in heaven that will last forever!

What is special about the prize Jesus wants to give us?

DEAR GOD, I want to live for Jesus all my
life and be a winner forever!
In Jesus' name. Amen.

June 27

Don't Stop Now!

Let us strip off anything that slows us down. . . .
Let us drop those sins that . . . trip us up. Let us run
with patience the race that God has set before us.
HEBREWS 12:1

If you run in a long race, you have to get rid of extra clothes that will slow you down. If you want to live for Jesus all your life, that's a very long race! So you need to get rid of sins that keep you from obeying him. Jesus wants to help you win. So you can ask him to help you stop doing bad things. And he will!

How can Jesus help you live for him all your life?

DEAR JESUS, I need your help to get rid of the bad things I do. Teach me how to follow you every day. Amen.

June 28

Jesus Prays for You

[Jesus prayed,] "I am not asking you to take [my friends] out of the world. But I am asking that you keep them safe. I am also praying for all people who will believe in me." JOHN 17:15, 20

When Jesus lived on earth, he prayed that God, his Father in heaven, would keep his friends safe. But do you know what's really exciting? Jesus didn't just pray for the friends he had then. He is also praying for *you!* He is praying for everyone who believes that he is God's Son.

Who are the people that Jesus prays for?

DEAR JESUS, I know you love me a lot because you pray for me. Thank you, Jesus. Amen.

June 29

God Will Be Our Guard

The Lord will go ahead of you. And he . . .
will protect you from behind. ISAIAH 52:12

Some countries have a king or queen who lives in a palace. There is a guard at every entrance to protect the king or queen. The guards don't let anyone go inside who doesn't belong there.

God is like a guard who protects us from every direction. He goes ahead of us and makes the way safe before we even get there! And he is behind us, so we don't need to be afraid of what's there either.

God never sleeps. How does that make him a good guard?

DEAR GOD, thank you for keeping me safe when I'm home with my family. Thank you for going with me and protecting me wherever I go. Amen.

June 30

God Stays the Same

[God is] the Creator of the sun, moon, and stars. God does not change like their shifting shadows.
JAMES 1:17

Have you ever used your hands and arms to make animal shapes on a wall? Shadows never stay the same, do they? The shapes are always changing. When it's cloudy, you can't even see your shadow. But do you know what? God is not like a shadow—he never changes! We can trust him to love us and take care of us all the time.

How is God different from a shadow?

DEAR GOD, I'm glad that you never change. I don't have to wonder if you're with me because I know you always are. Thanks, God! Amen.

July 1

Noah's World

The Lord saw that the human beings on the earth were very wicked. But Noah pleased the Lord.
GENESIS 6:5, 8

Way back when Noah was alive, God loved people just the way he loves you. He wanted people to love him back, but they didn't. They were very wicked—they did every bad thing you could think of, and more. But Noah wasn't like that. He was a good, kind man who pleased God.

When others do bad things, how can you be like Noah?

DEAR GOD, even when others fight and are unkind, help me to do good things. I want to please you like Noah did. Amen.

July 2

God Had a Plan

God said to Noah, "People have made the earth full of violence. . . . Build a boat . . . for yourself. I will bring a flood of water on the earth. I will destroy all living things." GENESIS 6:13-14, 17

God felt sad because people were mean to each other. He felt sad because they didn't even think about him anymore. But God was glad for Noah and his family. God told him to build a special boat called an "ark." Noah and his family were going to need that boat. That's because God was going to send a flood to cover the earth with water.

Why did God want Noah to build a boat?

DEAR GOD, thank you for coming up with a plan to keep Noah safe. I'm glad you knew that Noah loved you. I love you too! Amen.

July 3

The Big Boat

[God said,] "Make rooms in [the boat] and cover it inside and outside with tar. This is how big I want you to build the boat: 450 feet long, 75 feet wide and 45 feet high." GENESIS 6:14-15

Noah didn't have to wonder how to build the boat. God told him just how to do it! God also told him just how big to make the boat. God told him to make it very big! People must have thought Noah was crazy. There were no rivers or lakes or oceans nearby, so why did Noah need a boat? But Noah did everything God said to do.

Did Noah please God when he built the big boat?

DEAR GOD, help me to please you by learning what you want me to do each day. Amen.

July 4

God Thought of Everything!

*[God said,] "Make an opening around the top of the boat. . . .
Put a door in the side of the boat. Make an upper, middle and lower
deck in it."* GENESIS 6:16

The boat was going to be ready soon. It would have an opening all
around it to let in some light. There would be three decks, each with
many rooms. And there was going to be a door. Noah listened carefully
to God's directions. He wanted to be safe when the water came!

Why did Noah listen to God's directions?

DEAR GOD, you give good directions. Help me to listen carefully to your
words in the Bible so I'll be happy and safe. Amen.

July 5

A Full Boat

*[God told
Noah,] "You
must bring into
the boat two of every . . . kind of bird, animal and crawling thing. . . ."
Noah did everything that God commanded him.* GENESIS 6:19-20, 22

Could you fit two of every living thing in your house? The giraffes would go through the roof, and the elephants would crash through the floor! But the boat Noah built was big enough for him, his family, and all those animals, birds, and crawling things!

Why did God tell Noah to make the boat so big?

DEAR GOD, I'm glad Noah did everything you said. Help me to do that too. Amen.

July 6

Safe Inside

Noah and his wife, his sons . . . and their wives went into the boat.
One male and one female of every living thing came. . . .
Then the Lord closed the door. GENESIS 7:13, 16

Will the sun shine today? Will there be rain? Only God knows for sure! When God was ready to send rain soon, he told Noah to go into the boat. God took good care of Noah, his family, and all the other living things. He even closed the door of the boat behind them when they were safe inside!

How did God keep Noah safe?

DEAR GOD, thank you for taking care of Noah and for taking good care of me. Amen.

July 7

Water Everywhere!

Water flooded the earth for 40 days. . . .
The boat floated on the water. GENESIS 7:17-18

There was no dry land anywhere. The whole earth was covered with water. What do you suppose Noah was thinking about? Was he glad that he and his family were safe inside the boat? Was he glad that he had listened to God and obeyed him? Noah was probably very busy, too. He had a lot of animals to take care of!

Can you mark off 40 days on a calendar? That's a lot of rainy days!

DEAR GOD, I pray that you will always keep my family and me safe just as you kept Noah safe. Amen.

July 8

The Earth Gets Dry

God remembered Noah and all the . . . animals with him in the boat. God made a wind blow over the earth. . . . And the clouds in the sky stopped pouring down rain. GENESIS 8:1-2

Did God forget about the people and animals in the boat? No! God knew they couldn't stay in there forever. So he made the water start going away. Noah sent out a dove to see if the earth was dry. At first there was no dry place where the dove could land. But when the dove stayed away, Noah looked out and saw that the earth was dry again.

What did God do for Noah and the animals?

DEAR GOD, thank you for not forgetting about Noah. And thank you for never forgetting about me! Amen.

July 9

A Rainbow and a Promise

[God said,] "I will never again send another flood to destroy the earth. I have placed my rainbow in the clouds. It is a sign of my promise until the end of time." GENESIS 9:11, 13

Noah and his family hadn't stood on dry land for over a year! Now Noah thanked God for keeping him and his family safe. God promised that he would never cover the earth with water again. Then God put a rainbow in the sky—just like we see when the sun comes out after the rain.

What should you think about when you see a rainbow?

DEAR GOD, thank you for rainbows and for your promise never to cover the earth with water again. Amen.

July 10

Time to Move

The Lord said to Abram, "Leave your country, your relatives and your father's family. Go to the land I will show you." GENESIS 12:1

Many years after the Flood, a man named Abram lived in the town of Haran. God told Abram it was time to move. But guess what—God didn't give him any directions! God wanted Abram to trust him and believe that God would show him the way. Abram did believe. He packed his things and got ready to move with his wife, Sarai, and his nephew, Lot.

Why did Abram pack his things? Did you or one of your friends ever move?

DEAR GOD, help me to trust you the way Abram did. In Jesus' name. Amen.

July 11

A New Place to Live

The Lord said [to Abram], "I will give this land to your descendants."
GENESIS 12:7

There were no airplanes or cars yet. So Abram, his family, and their helpers had to walk to their new home! They took their camels and sheep and donkeys with them. They rolled up their tents and took them along too. Every night they slept in the tents. Finally they came to the land where God wanted them to live. God promised to give the land to  Abram's children and grandchildren and all of their children's children.

What special promise did God make to Abram?

DEAR GOD, thank you for giving Abram a place to live. Thank you for my home too. Amen.

July 12

Let's Not Fight

Abram said to Lot, "There should be no arguing between you and me." GENESIS 13:8

Abram and Lot both had a lot of sheep and cows. They had just one problem—there wasn't enough grass or water for all of the animals. So Abram's helpers began to fight with Lot's helpers. Each one wanted the best land for his animals. But then Abram told Lot that they should keep their animals in different places. He told Lot to choose the place he wanted.

What can you do when you need to end a fight?

DEAR GOD, I'm sorry about the fights I've had. Show me how to get along with everyone. Amen.

July 13

Lot Needs Help

[Lot] moved very near to Sodom. Now the people of Sodom were . . . always sinning against the Lord. GENESIS 13:12-13

L ot thought he was getting away from fights. But he did not choose a good place to live. The people around him did bad things. Why, the king even had fights with kings from other countries! One day people from another country took Lot and his family away. When Abram heard about it, he went to help bring them back again.

Do the people around you ever do bad things?

DEAR GOD, thank you for sending help when my friends are fighting and doing other bad things. Amen.

July 14

Too Many to Count

*God said [to Abram],
". . . There are so many stars
you cannot count them. And
your descendants will be too
many to count."* GENESIS 15:5

Abram was old, but he and his wife
had no children. So he talked to God
about it. God made a special promise to
Abram. He said Abram would have such a
big family that he wouldn't be able to count all
the people! It would be like trying to count the
stars. Abram would have many descendants—
children and grandchildren and all of
their children's children.

***Why did God want Abram
to look at the stars?***

DEAR GOD, thank you for
promising Abram a big family.
Thank you for my family.
Amen.

July 15

New Names

[God said,] "Obey me and do what is right.
I am changing your name from Abram to Abraham.
The name of Sarai, your wife . . . will be Sarah."
GENESIS 17:1, 5, 15

God gave Abram the name Abraham because he was going to become a father. Someday his family would live in many places. Sarai became Sarah, which means "princess." She was going to become the mother of Abraham's son Isaac.

God was planning good things for Abraham. All that God asked Abraham to do was obey him.

What did God ask Abraham to do?

DEAR GOD, I know you plan good things for me just like you did for Abraham. Help me to obey you. Amen.

July 16

God Can Do Anything!

[Sarah] laughed to herself, "My husband and I are too old to have a baby." Then the Lord said to Abraham, ". . . Is anything too hard for the Lord? No!" GENESIS 18:12-14

Abraham and Sarah were old enough to be great-grandparents. They were around 100 years old! People who are that old usually can't do any work, and they certainly are too old to have children. So Sarah laughed when God said they would have a baby. But nothing is too hard for God. He helped Abraham and Sarah become the mom and dad of baby Isaac!

Why was it so special for Abraham and Sarah to become a mom and dad?

DEAR GOD, I'm glad nothing is too hard for you to do. Amen.

July 17

Moses Runs Away

One day [Moses] visited his people, the Hebrews. He saw that they were forced to work very hard. He saw an Egyptian beating a Hebrew man. EXODUS 2:11

Long after baby Isaac grew up, people from his family moved to Egypt. That's where baby Moses was born. Baby Moses' sister helped to keep him safe from a mean king. But when Moses grew up, the king and the Egyptian people were still mean. Moses tried to help his people, but it didn't work. So Moses ran away and began taking care of sheep.

Why did Moses run away?

DEAR GOD, I know you don't want me to play with kids who are mean. Show me when it's OK to run away from them. Amen.

July 18

A Burning Bush

The angel of the Lord appeared to Moses in flames of fire coming out of a bush. EXODUS 3:2

People need to be careful around fire, don't they? Even the little flame on a candle gets very hot. You need to blow it out before the candle burns up. Well, Moses came to a bush that was on fire, but it didn't burn up! God talked to him from the bush. God cared about his people in Egypt. He told Moses to go back there and take the people away from the mean king.

What did God tell Moses from the burning bush?

DEAR GOD, thank you for caring about your people. Help me to care about my friends too. Amen.

July 19

Moses Doesn't Give Up

"Go back to Pharaoh," the Lord told Moses. "Tell him, 'The Lord . . . demands that you let his people go.'" EXODUS 9:1

The mean king of Egypt was called Pharaoh. It was hard for Moses to talk to him. So God let Moses' brother, Aaron, go with him. They had to go to Pharaoh over and over again. Each time they went, they told him to let God's people go. After God sent many troubles to Egypt, Pharaoh finally let Moses take God's people away.

What did Moses have to do over and over again?

DEAR GOD, when you want me to do something that's hard, please help me to be like Moses and not give up. Amen.

July 20

No One Gets Wet!

The Lord drove back the sea with a strong east wind. And so he made the sea become dry ground. The water was split. EXODUS 14:21

Moses was so excited to be leading God's people out of Egypt! But soon things began to look bad again. There was a big sea in front of them. And coming after them was the mean king with his army. But God told Moses what to do. And God made the water split so the people could walk right across the sea on dry ground!

What problems were God's people facing?

DEAR GOD, you can do anything, so
I know you can take care of my
problems. Thank you!
Amen.

July 21

Ten Special Rules

The Lord said to Moses, ". . . I will give you two stone tablets. On these are the . . . commandments. I have written these to teach the people." EXODUS 24:12

Do you have rules at your house that help you get along with your family? Rules are good for that! God gave Moses some rules called commandments. They teach people how to live. God's rules tell us to worship God every week on his special day and to treat our parents with respect. They tell us not to worship fake gods, steal, or tell lies.

What are some of God's special rules?

DEAR GOD, thank you for your rules, which teach us the right way to live. Amen.

July 22

God Sees What's Inside

People look at the outside of a person, but the Lord looks at the heart. I SAMUEL 16:7

God's people were living in the land Moses had led them to. Now God told Samuel that one of Jesse's sons should be king. Samuel thought God had chosen the oldest, tallest, best-looking son. But God had chosen David, who loved God with all his heart. He was the youngest and not the tallest, but he would be the best king.

Who knows what we're like inside—how we think and feel?

DEAR GOD, you know what I'm really like, just as you knew all about David. Thank you for understanding me. Amen.

July 23

Food for David's Brothers

Jesse said to his son David, ". . . See how your brothers are. . . . They are fighting against the Philistines." I SAMUEL 17:17-19

David wasn't the king yet. He was still living with his father and taking care of sheep. One day his father asked him to take food to his brothers. They were in the army, waiting to fight enemy soldiers. David probably would have liked to stay with the sheep. But he did what his father asked. He left the next morning.

If you don't feel like doing what your mom or dad asks you to do, what should you do then?

DEAR GOD, help me to please you by doing what I'm asked even when I don't want to. Amen.

July 24

"I Dare You!"

[Goliath] said, "Today I stand and dare the army of Israel! Send one of your men to fight me!"
1 SAMUEL 17:10

Goliath was a giant—he was over nine feet tall! That's about how tall you'd be if you stood on your dad's shoulders! Goliath wanted to fight God's people—the army of Israel. He shouted, "I dare you to send one man to fight with me!" The men in the army of Israel were afraid. No one dared to fight Goliath.

Why were the men of Israel afraid to fight Goliath?

DEAR GOD, sometimes I don't dare to face my troubles because they seem as big as giants. Please show me how to handle them. Amen.

July 25

A Brave Young Man

David asked the men who stood near him, ". . . Why does [Goliath] think he can speak against the armies of the living God?" 1 SAMUEL 17:26

David was just visiting his big brothers in the army. He wasn't even a soldier. But David was the only one who was brave enough to even *think* about fighting with Goliath, the giant. David knew that God would help his people. But David's oldest brother was upset with him. His brother said, "You should be home taking care of your sheep."

Who was brave—David or his big brothers?

DEAR GOD, I want to be brave like David and trust you to help me. Amen.

July 26

A Little Boy and a Big God

[David said to Goliath,] "You have spoken out against [the Lord]. Today the Lord will give you to me." I SAMUEL 17:45-46

Goliath said bad things about God and his people. So David knew that God would help him win the fight with Goliath. In fact, God had already helped David fight a lion and a bear! David picked up five stones and put one in his sling. He swung the leather strap around and around until the stone flew out and hit the mean giant. No one had to worry about Goliath after that.

How did David know that God would help him?

DEAR GOD, I'm not very big, but you're a big God. I know you'll always take care of me. Amen.

July 27

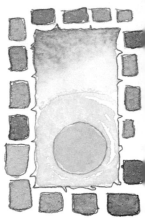

David Is Kind

David said, "Don't be afraid! I've asked you to come so that I can be kind to you. This is because of my promise to your father Jonathan."
2 SAMUEL 9:7

When Saul was the king, David and the king's son, Jonathan, were good friends. Now Saul and Jonathan were no longer living, but David learned that Jonathan had a son. This young man's feet had been hurt, and David wanted to help him. He gave Jonathan's son the land that had belonged to his grandfather. David also let the young man live right at the palace!

What did David do for Jonathan's son?

DEAR GOD, show me how to be kind to someone today or tomorrow. Amen.

July 28

David, the King

When the evil spirit . . . entered Saul, David would take his harp and play. Now Saul was dead. The men of Judah . . . appointed David king. 1 SAMUEL 16:23; 2 SAMUEL 1:1; 2:4

David played his harp for King Saul. But Saul became very jealous of David and tried to hurt him. David had to run away for a while, but God kept him safe. After Saul died, David became the next king. That's just the way God had planned it to be way back when David was a shepherd boy.

What did David do before he became a king?

DEAR GOD, you know what I'm going to do when I grow up. So I'll trust you to make things happen the way you've planned. Amen.

July 29

Songs about God

The Lord is my shepherd. I have everything I need. He gives me rest in green pastures. He leads me to calm water. PSALM 23:1-2

When David was young, he was a good shepherd boy. He led his sheep to green pastures where there was plenty of grass to eat. He also led them to quiet streams of water where they wouldn't be afraid to drink. David knew that God took care of him just as he took care of his sheep. So David wrote songs about God. He called God his shepherd.

Why did David call God his shepherd?

DEAR GOD, thank you for being my shepherd and giving me everything I need. In Jesus' name. Amen.

July 30

My Shepherd Is Nearby

I will not be afraid. For you are close beside me. And you are guarding and guiding all the way. PSALM 23:4

Sometimes sheep get hurt or lost, and wild animals are nearby. But sheep don't need to be afraid because their shepherd is nearby too. David would always guard his sheep to keep them away from trouble. And if they got stuck somewhere, he would get them out and guide them to a safe place. David knew that God would do that for him, too. So he wrote about it in his song.

When you know that God is nearby, how does that help you not to feel afraid?

DEAR GOD, thank you for keeping me away from trouble and for guiding me to safe places. Amen.

July 31

Safe All Night

"I am the Gate for the sheep," [Jesus] said.
JOHN 10:7

God's Son, Jesus, came to show us what God is like. Jesus said that he is our shepherd, and we're his sheep. A shepherd keeps his sheep safe inside their pen at night by placing himself at the entrance. He is the gate! The sheep can't get out and wander off by themselves to places where it wouldn't be safe. And nothing can get inside to hurt the sheep.

How does Jesus keep us safe?

DEAR JESUS, I'm so glad you're my shepherd! Keep me safe all through the night. Amen.

August 1

Take Them Away

[The] king of Babylon came to Jerusalem and surrounded it with his army.
DANIEL 1:1

Long before Jesus came to earth, a king and his army came to the city of Jerusalem. They were from the country of Babylon, and they took many of the people away from Jerusalem. The king of Babylon told his army leader to take the best young men from the best families.

These young men had to go to Babylon to live. But even in that place far away, God took care of them.

What did many of the young men in Jerusalem have to do?

DEAR GOD, thank you for going with me even when I have to go to places where I don't want to go. Amen.

August 2

No, Thank You!

Daniel decided not to eat the king's food and wine.
DANIEL 1:8

When you go to someone else's house, do your mom and dad tell you to be polite and eat the food? They probably do! But Daniel had a good reason for not eating. He and some other young men had been taken to Babylon. The people there worshiped fake gods, and the food on the table had been offered to those gods. Daniel and his friends would be disobeying God if they ate the food.

Why was it OK for Daniel not to eat the king's food?

DEAR GOD, teach me to obey you even while I'm eating. In Jesus' name. Amen.

August 3

More Vegetables, Please!

*Daniel said to the guard,
". . . Don't give us anything but
vegetables to eat and water to drink."*
DANIEL 1:12

Daniel wanted to please God and not eat the king's food. So Daniel talked to the guard who was feeding him and his friends. He asked for vegetables and water for ten days. Then the guard was to see whether Daniel and his friends were healthier than those who ate the king's food. Sure enough, Daniel and his friends were the healthiest young men!

What made Daniel and his friends so healthy?

DEAR GOD, thank you for knowing what's best for me. Amen.

August 4

The Best Students

Every time the king asked [Daniel and his friends] about something important, they showed much wisdom and understanding.
DANIEL 1:20

Daniel and his friends were living in the country where they had been taken. They had to learn many new things. God helped them learn and become very wise. When the king asked them questions, he could tell that they knew a lot. In fact, they knew more than any of the other people around the king!

Who helped Daniel and his friends learn new things?

DEAR GOD, there are so many new things to learn every day. Will you help me learn everything you want me to know? Thanks, God! Amen.

August 5

What Was My Dream?

Daniel asked [the king] to give him some more time. Then he would tell the king what he had dreamed. DANIEL 2:16

If you have a dream, no one else can tell you what it was about, can they? But that's what the king wanted his helpers to do. When they couldn't, the king wanted to get rid of them. Then Daniel came along and asked for more time. What do you think

Daniel did during that time? He asked his friends to pray! Then God showed Daniel what the king's dream was.

What wise thing did Daniel ask his friends to do?

DEAR GOD, thank you for helping Daniel. I'm glad that I can always pray when I need help too. Amen.

August 6

A New Job

The king . . . put Daniel in charge of all the wise men of Babylon.
DANIEL 2:48

The king was pleased that Daniel could tell him about his dream. Daniel said that it was God who helped him do it. Then the king knew how great God is. And he knew that God helped Daniel to be very wise. So the king made Daniel the most important wise man in Babylon! He gave Daniel many gifts, too. Daniel asked if his friends Shadrach, Meshach, and Abednego could help him. The king said yes.

Why did good things happen to Daniel?

DEAR GOD, thank you for the good things you did for Daniel. Thank you for all the good things you have planned for me. Amen.

August 7

A Gold Statue

Shadrach, Meshach and Abednego . . .
do not worship the gold statue.
DANIEL 3:12

The king of Babylon wanted his leaders to worship a statue made from gold. He said they would hear music playing. That's when they should bow down in front of the statue. They should worship it as if it were a god. Well, Daniel's three friends were there. But they knew it was wrong to worship a fake god. So they turned the other way. They would worship no one but God in heaven.

Why did Daniel's three friends turn away from the statue?

DEAR GOD, I love you just like Daniel's friends did. Help me to never worship anyone but you. In Jesus' name. Amen.

August 8

An Angry King

[The king said,] "If you do not worship [the statue I made], you will be thrown quickly into the blazing furnace." DANIEL 3:15

Now the king was angry. He gave Daniel's friends another chance to do what he said. But if they didn't obey this time, they would be thrown into a hot furnace. Well, they still did not obey the king. They knew that it was more important to obey God and that he could keep them safe. Even if he didn't, they'd obey him anyway!

Why was it OK not to obey the king?

DEAR GOD, no one is more important than you. Teach me to always obey you. Amen.

August 9

And Then There Were Four

The king told the soldiers to throw [Shadrach, Meshach, and Abednego] into the blazing furnace. DANIEL 3:20

The king was really angry now. He had his soldiers throw Daniel's friends into a very hot fire. How many men were thrown into the fire? There were three, weren't there? But guess how many men the king saw in the furnace. He saw four! And they were walking around! Then the king knew that God was keeping the three men safe.

Who kept Daniel's friends safe?

DEAR GOD, no one but you could have kept Daniel's friends safe. Help me to trust you just as they did. Amen.

August 10

A King Praises God

[The king] said, "Praise the God of Shadrach, Meshach and Abednego. Their God has sent his angel and saved [them] from the fire!" DANIEL 3:28

When Daniel's friends came out of the fire, they weren't hurt at all! The king wasn't angry anymore. Instead, he began to praise God. Do you know what else he did? He made a new law. This law said that no one could say anything bad about God. Anyone who did would be in big trouble.

Why do you think the king made the new law?

DEAR GOD, thank you for helping Daniel's friends do what was right. If they hadn't, the king might never have learned about you. Amen.

August 11

"I Want It Now!"

Jesus said, "A man had two sons. The younger son said to his father, 'Give me my share of the property.'"
LUKE 15:11-12

When Jesus lived on earth, he told a story about a son who wanted to leave home. The son thought he'd enjoy getting away from his father and his older brother. But he didn't just want to leave. He also wanted his share of all that his father owned. The father should have been able to keep what he had until he died. But he divided up everything and gave each son his share.

How can you tell that the younger son thought only about himself?

DEAR GOD, thank you for everything my family gives me. I don't want to leave home for a long time yet! Amen.

August 12

Leaving Home

The younger son gathered up all that was his and left. He traveled far away to another country. There he wasted his money in foolish living.
LUKE 15:13

The younger son left home feeling happy that he had gotten his way. He probably didn't even see the tears in his father's eyes. Well, the young man did have a good time for a while. But he wasn't very wise about the way he spent his money. He didn't notice how quickly it was disappearing.

Do you think the young man should have left home? Why or why not?

DEAR GOD, sometimes I do things that aren't very wise. Help me to learn what I need to know from my family before I grow up and leave home. Amen.

August 13

Out of Money

The land became very dry, and there was no rain. There was not enough food to eat anywhere in the country. The son was hungry and needed money. LUKE 15:14

The young man's money was gone because he had spent it on things that didn't please God. And now there wasn't enough food to eat in the country where he was living. So he got a job feeding pigs. It was hard, dirty work. But he had gotten his way, hadn't he?

Do you suppose things turned out the way the young man thought they would?

DEAR GOD, sometimes I do things I shouldn't do. I think everything will be OK, but I get myself into a mess. Help me not to keep doing that. In Jesus' name. Amen.

August 14

Pig Food

The son was so hungry that he was willing to eat the food the pigs were eating. But no one gave him anything.
LUKE 15:16

The younger son in Jesus' story became very hungry. He would have eaten pig food, but no one would even let him have that. What a hard time he was having! He had to feed those fat little pigs so they would get fatter. But he was starving. Was he having a better time than when he lived at home? No way!

What do you think the younger son was learning?

DEAR GOD, teach me to talk to you about the things I want to do. You can keep me from having to learn everything the hard way. Thanks, God. Amen.

August 15

Good Thinking

[The son thought,] "I will leave and return to my father. I'll say to him: Father, I have sinned against God and have done wrong to you." LUKE 15:18

As the son started his trip back home, he wasn't happy like he had been when he left. He knew he had done things that were wrong, and he was sorry. He would ask God to forgive him. And he would ask his father to forgive him too.

What was the son thinking about on his way home?

DEAR GOD, I'm sorry about the wrong things I've done. I want you to forgive me, and I want my family to forgive me. In Jesus' name. Amen.

August 16

Home Again!

While the son was still a long way off, his father saw him coming. . . . So the father ran to him, and hugged and kissed him. LUKE 15:20

The younger son in Jesus' story hadn't even gotten home yet when he saw his father. Do you know what the father was doing? Looking for his son! He ran to meet the young man and gave him a hug! The son told him how sorry he was for the wrong things he had done. Suddenly, the young man felt happy again. He was home, and his father still loved him!

Why was the young man happy again?

DEAR GOD, thank you for being like the father in Jesus' story. Amen.

August 17

A Happy Ending

[The father said,] "My son was . . . lost, but now he is found!" So they began to celebrate. LUKE 15:24

The father in Jesus' story was very happy to have his missing son home again. He had his helpers bring out new clothes and sandals for the young man. He asked them to fix lots of good food so he could have a big party. The father was so happy that he wanted everyone else to be happy along with him!

How did the father welcome his son home?

DEAR GOD, I'm so glad that you are ready to welcome me just like the father in Jesus' story. Help me to come and talk to you often. In Jesus' name. Amen.

August 18

The Lost Coin

Jesus told them this story: "Suppose a woman has ten silver coins, but she loses one of them."
LUKE 15:3, 8

Did you ever lose something? Were you upset? If it was a favorite toy or a gift from someone, you probably felt very bad.

Jesus told a story about a woman who got married and received a gift of ten silver coins. She felt bad when she lost one of the special coins. That's how God feels if you don't love him. He feels as if he lost the gift of your love.

How does it feel to lose something special?

DEAR GOD, I'm glad that I am special to you and that you don't want to lose the gift of my love. Amen.

August 19

The Search Goes On

[Jesus said,] "She will light a lamp and clean the house. She will look carefully for the coin until she finds it." LUKE 15:8

There were no electric lights in Bible times. So a woman who lost a coin would need to light a lamp the way we light candles. She would sweep her floor and keep looking until she found her coin. That's how God keeps looking for us when we forget about him.

Would a woman who lost a coin give up looking for it?

DEAR GOD, thank you for caring about me even more than a woman cares about her lost coin. Amen.

August 20

Joy in Heaven

When she finds [her coin], she will call her friends and neighbors and say, "Be happy with me . . . !" LUKE 15:9

A woman who found her coin would tell her friends about it so they could be happy too. Jesus said there is a time when this is what it's like in heaven. All of the angels are happy along with God. When does this happen? It's when someone who has done bad things changes the way he or she lives. The person stops doing bad things and begins loving God.

What makes God and all of his angels happy?

DEAR JESUS, thank you for telling the story about the lost coin. I like knowing what makes everyone in heaven happy. Amen.

August 21

A Message for Jesus

Two sisters sent a message to Jesus. It said,
"Sir, your good friend is very sick."
JOHN 11:3

Mary and Martha lived in Bethany with their brother, Lazarus. Jesus liked to visit them—they were all good friends. When Lazarus became very sick, the two sisters wanted Jesus to know. They were sure that he would come right away to help their brother. So they had someone take a message to him.

What did Mary and Martha want Jesus to do?

DEAR JESUS, whenever I know someone who is sick, help me remember to tell you about it. Amen.

August 22

A Reason for Waiting

[Jesus] stayed where he was for the next two days. Then he told [his disciples] plainly, "Lazarus is dead. . . . This will give you another chance to believe in me. Come, let's go to him." JOHN 11:6, 14-15

Jesus waited to go to his friend until he had died. Why? Because Jesus knew he could still help. And he wanted everyone else to see what he could do. That would teach people who he was. After all, no one but God's Son could help someone who had died.

Why didn't Jesus go to Lazarus right away?

DEAR JESUS, sometimes I have to wait for an answer to my prayers. Help me to believe that you always have a good reason for making me wait. Amen.

August 23

Jesus Finally Comes

Jesus told [Martha], "I am the resurrection and the life. Anyone who believes in me, even though he dies, will live again." JOHN 11:25

Lazarus had been dead for four days. Martha went out to meet Jesus. She told him that if he had been there, her brother would not have died. Jesus said that Lazarus would live again. Martha believed that would be true in heaven someday. But not everyone believed that. So Jesus was ready to do something very special to help them believe.

What did Jesus tell Martha about her brother?

DEAR JESUS, thank you that I can believe in you and live in heaven with you after I die. Amen.

August 24

Jesus Cries with His Friends

Jesus saw [Mary] crying. . . . He was very moved and deeply troubled. JOHN 11:33

Martha went back to get her sister, Mary. When Mary came out to the place where Jesus was, he saw that she was crying. The other people with her were crying too. Their tears made him feel sad. And when they took him to the place where his friend Lazarus was buried, Jesus cried too.

Jesus cared a lot about his friends, didn't he?

How did Jesus feel when he saw how sad Mary and her friends were?

DEAR JESUS, thank you for understanding how I feel. Thank you for knowing what it's like to feel sad. Amen.

August 25

Alive Again!

[Jesus] shouted, "Lazarus, come out!" And Lazarus come out! JOHN 11:43-44

Lazarus had been dead for four days. But when Jesus called his name, he came out of the cave where he had been buried! He was wrapped in cloth, so Jesus told the people to unwrap him. What an exciting moment that must have been! Many people believed then that Jesus was God's Son. This happened a little while before Jesus died and came back to life again.

Why did many people believe in Jesus?

DEAR JESUS, thank you for your power and your love. Thank you for helping people believe in you. Amen.

August 26

Full of Joy

[Jesus said,] "You have never asked for anything in my name. Ask and you will receive. And your joy will be the fullest joy." JOHN 16:24

Did you ever hear someone say, "Just mention my name"? Maybe your mom had a friend who knew a car dealer. When she mentioned her friend's name to him, he helped her find a good car. Well, we know a very special name—Jesus! We often end our prayers by saying, "In Jesus' name. Amen." God gives us the things Jesus wants us to have, and we're happy—we're full of joy!

Why should you pray in Jesus' name?

DEAR GOD, thanks for letting me use Jesus' name when I talk to you. Please give me everything I need for today. I pray this in Jesus' name. Amen.

August 27

New Bodies

When Jesus gives us new life, our bodies will be different. They will never die.
I CORINTHIANS 15:42

Think about some things you know about your body: It's growing; it needs food; it gets tired; sometimes it gets hurt or sick. If you believe in God's Son, Jesus, God promises to give you a new body! You probably won't get it for a long time. But someday you will go to live with Jesus in heaven and get your new body. It will never get tired or sick, and it will never die—it will last forever!

How will your new body be different from the one you have now?

DEAR GOD, thank you for the body I have now. And thanks for the new one that will be even better! In Jesus' name. Amen.

August 28

A Gift That Saves Us

You did not save yourselves. It was a gift from God. EPHESIANS 2:8

When you go for a swim, you never want to be alone. You want someone nearby who can save you if you start to sink. The Bible tells about another way that we all need to be saved. We need to be saved from our sins. Sins are the bad things we do. We can't save ourselves, but *God* wants to save us! He helps us trust in his Son, Jesus. What a wonderful gift from God!

How does God help to save you from your sins?

DEAR GOD, thank you for helping me trust in your Son, Jesus. I'm glad that your gift of trust will save me from my sins. Amen.

August 29

God's Peace

The peace that God gives is so great that we cannot understand it.
PHILIPPIANS 4:7

Perhaps you've heard your mom and dad say, "We'd like a little peace and quiet, please." They mean that they don't want their family to fight or shout angry words—or get the cat upset!

God gives us his peace when we trust his Son, Jesus. If we keep thinking about Jesus, we won't worry. We'll feel peaceful inside, and we won't understand why we're getting along so well with everyone!

How do we get God's peace?

DEAR GOD, thank you for giving me your peace when I trust Jesus. In his name. Amen.

August 30

A Gift for Jesus

[Jesus prayed,] "Father, I want these people that you have given me to be with me in every place I am." JOHN 17:24

God gives you everything you need. He gives you a family and friends. He gives you his peace and his love. But did you know that God gives gifts to his Son, Jesus, too? If you love Jesus, *you* are a gift from God to his Son! Jesus is very pleased to have the gift of your love. Someday you'll see him sitting on a throne in heaven. You'll see how wonderful he is, and he will always let you be with him.

How can you be a gift from God to Jesus?

DEAR JESUS, I love you. I want to see you on your throne in heaven someday. In your name I pray. Amen.

August 31

The Helper Comes

[Jesus said,] "The Helper will teach you everything. . . . This Helper is the Holy Spirit whom the Father will send in my name." JOHN 14:26

When Jesus lived on earth, he told about a Helper. Jesus said that God was going to send the Helper as a gift. This Helper has now come in Jesus' name. That means he has come to help us just as Jesus would if he were still living here. The Helper is the Holy Spirit. Just like Jesus is God, the Holy Spirit is God. He teaches you everything God wants you to know.

Who is the Helper God sent?

DEAR GOD, thank you for the Holy Spirit, who teaches me about you. Amen.

September 1

You're Wonderful, God!

Why am I so sad? Why am I so upset? I should put my hope in God. I should keep praising him.
PSALM 42:5

When things go wrong, you might feel sad and upset. You might just think about yourself. But what if you thought about God instead? You could praise him by telling him that you know how great he is. You could tell him that you know he can help you. And you could sing songs of praise to him. Soon you wouldn't feel so sad or upset!

What are some ways to praise God? Why should you praise him?

DEAR GOD, I praise you for being so wonderful. I praise you for always being able to help me. Amen.

September 2

Morning and Night

It is good to praise the Lord. . . . It is good to tell of your love in the morning and of your loyalty at night. PSALM 92:1-2

Did you know that you can praise God when you're all alone? A good place to praise him is right in your own bed. You can tell God that he is wonderful. You'll want to praise him for his love. And you can praise him for being loyal to you—for always being with you and listening to your prayers. The Bible says that it's good to praise God, and you can do it any time of the day.

When can you praise God?

DEAR GOD, I'm glad that I can praise you all the time, even when I'm alone in bed. In Jesus' name. Amen.

September 3

Angel Praise

*The angels said in a loud voice:
"[Jesus] is worthy to receive . . . honor,
glory, and praise!"* REVELATION 5:12

Is it just people who praise God? No! Angels praise him too. Is it just God the Father who is good enough to receive praise? No! Jesus, who is God the Son, deserves to be honored, to be given special attention for who he is, and to be praised. When you praise Jesus, you are worshiping him right along with the angels!

What can you and the angels do together?

DEAR JESUS, you are awesome! You are God's very own Son, and you love me. I praise you for that. Amen.

September 4

Praise the King

God is King of all the earth.
So sing a song of praise to him.
PSALM 47:7

Do you like to paint pictures of the world God made? There are many things to paint, aren't there? After God made the world, he could have left and never come back. But he didn't. He stayed as the king who rules "all the earth." He is in charge of everything! That's a very good reason to praise him.

What is God in charge of?

DEAR GOD, I praise you for all the things you made. I praise you because you're in charge of everything! Amen.

September 5

Eating and Praising

The believers . . . [were] happy to share their food. . . . They praised God, and all the people liked them. ACTS 2:46-47

People who believe in Jesus are called "believers." Some of the first believers met together in their homes. They liked to eat together and share their food. They liked to praise God together too. Their neighbors saw how happy they were and how much they loved God. The neighbors liked them.

Why did the neighbors like the people who believed in Jesus?

DEAR GOD, I want to praise you with other believers. And I want my neighbors to see how much I love you. In Jesus' name. Amen.

September 6

Praising God with Music

Praise the Lord! Praise him with trumpet blasts. . . . Praise him with tambourines and dancing. . . . Praise him with loud cymbals.
PSALM 150:1, 3-5

When you hear music, do you like to clap your hands? Do you like to dance to the beat of the music? Do you like to play a musical instrument or sing?

Music makes us feel happy, doesn't it? When we praise God with music, he feels happy too.

You can sing and play songs about God at church. You can do it at home, too!

What favorite praise song can you play for God right now?

DEAR GOD, thank you for songs and musical instruments that help me praise you. Amen.

September 7

Songs at Church

Come before [the Lord] with singing. Come into his courtyards with songs of praise. PSALM 100:2, 4

In Bible times people often went to a beautiful building called the "temple." They would gather in its big, outdoor courtyards to worship God. The Bible says that the people were to sing songs of praise there. Even though they couldn't see God, it would be just as if they were standing right in front of him. And that's how it is when we go to church!

What should you do with your friends at church?

DEAR GOD, I like to sing songs and praise you with my friends at church. In Jesus' name. Amen.

September 8

Singing in Jail

Paul and Silas were thrown into jail. About midnight [they]
were praying and singing songs to God. ACTS 16:23, 25

Some people threw Paul and Silas into jail for teaching others about
Jesus. The two men could have cried or screamed or grumbled, but
they didn't. In the middle of the night, they prayed and sang to God! Then
there was an earthquake. The man in charge of the jail was glad Paul and
Silas didn't run away. They helped him and his family learn about Jesus.

Where did Paul and Silas praise God?

DEAR GOD, help me to praise you
even when I feel like grumbling or
screaming.
Amen.

September 9

Hard Times

*No blossoms or fruit will be left . . . and the
cattle barns will be empty. Even when all this happens,
I will rejoice in the Lord. . . . [He] is my strength.*
HABAKKUK 3:17-19

There would be no fruit to eat and no cows to give milk. But
Habakkuk was still going to praise God for being his strength. Kids
have hard times too. One has no money. Another gets hurt. You break a
toy. A friend gets sick. When these things happen, you can still praise God
for the strength he gives.

What can you say to God when you're having a hard time?

DEAR GOD, I praise you for giving me strength when I'm having
a hard time. Amen.

September 10

A New Song

Sing to the Lord a new song.
Tell the nations, "The Lord
is king." PSALM 96:1, 10

When David was a shepherd boy, he wrote and sang songs to God. Then David became a king, and he wrote and sang new songs of praise.

King David was an important person. He was the leader of a whole nation, or country. Other nations had kings too. But David said to tell all nations that God is the most important King. He is King over all other kings!

What words can you use to make up a song about God?

DEAR GOD, I praise you for being the King of all the people in the world. Amen.

September 11

Quiet Praise

Sing and make music in your hearts to the Lord. EPHESIANS 5:19

What are some things you can do when you can't talk out loud? Can you think happy thoughts? Can you talk quietly to God in your mind? Can you remember a fun time you had? Sure you can. You can also sing to Jesus! When you think about the words and music of a praise song, you are making music in your heart. Try doing that the next time you have to wait in a line.

What song might you think about when you want to make music in your heart?

DEAR GOD, thank you for hearing my praise songs even when I can't sing them out loud. Amen.

September 12

A Happy Song

Hannah said: "The Lord has filled my heart with joy. . . . I am glad because you have helped me!" I SAMUEL 2:1

Hannah was so happy that she just had to talk to God! After all, he was the one who had made her happy. She had prayed for a son, and God had helped her have baby Samuel! Hannah had said that if God helped her have a baby, she would have him become a full-time worker for God. Well, Samuel was a young boy now. Hannah was praising God because it was time for her son to begin working for him.

Why was Hannah so happy?

DEAR GOD, I praise you for all the things you've done for me. Thank you for making me happy. Amen.

A LITTLE MAN WALKS TALL

September 13

Too Short to See

[Zacchaeus] wanted to see who Jesus was. LUKE 19:3

Did you ever try to watch a parade? That can be hard to do when there are a lot of big people around. Well, Zacchaeus was a grown-up man who wanted to see Jesus as he came through town. But Zacchaeus was shorter than most grown-ups. So he had to figure out a way to see Jesus. And he did—he climbed a tree!

Was seeing Jesus important to Zacchaeus? How do you know?

DEAR JESUS, you're in heaven now, so I can't see you. But I want to learn all about you. Help me to find lots of ways to do that. Amen.

September 14

A Very Special Guest

Jesus . . . looked up and saw Zacchaeus in the tree. He said to him, "Zacchaeus, hurry and come down! I must stay at your house today."
LUKE 19:5

Wow! What a surprise for Zacchaeus! He had found a place where he could see *Jesus*. But most likely he never thought Jesus would see *him!* And he certainly didn't expect Jesus to come home with him! But when Jesus told Zacchaeus to "hurry and come down," that's what the little man did.

How did Jesus surprise Zacchaeus?

DEAR JESUS, I feel as if you have come to stay at my house too. That's because I can talk to you anytime. I like that! Amen.

September 15

Jesus and a Sinner

The people . . . began to complain, "Look at the kind of man Jesus stays with. Zacchaeus is a sinner!" LUKE 19:7

People knew that Zacchaeus did bad things. He lied to them and stole money from them. His job was to collect tax money, but he asked for more money than he should have. And he kept the extra for himself. That made the people angry. They called Zacchaeus a sinner. But Jesus knew about the little man's sins. In fact, Jesus said he came to help people like Zacchaeus.

Jesus knew what Zacchaeus was like, so why did Jesus go home with him?

DEAR JESUS, I'm glad that you love me even though I do bad things. Please help me to do what's right. Amen.

September 16

I'm Really Sorry!

Zacchaeus said to the Lord, "I will give half of my money to the poor. If I have cheated anyone, I will pay that person back four times more!" LUKE 19:8

Some people are so good that when we're with them, we just want to do good things. Maybe your grandpa or your Sunday school teacher is like that. But no one is as good as Jesus. So when he went home with Zacchaeus, the little man wanted to stop doing bad things right away! He was sorry for his sins. And he showed it by telling Jesus about the good things he was going to do.

How did Jesus help Zacchaeus?

DEAR JESUS, thank you for being so good and for helping me want to be good too. Amen.

September 17

Giving Thanks

Give thanks to the Lord because he is good. His love continues forever. PSALM 136:1

Did you ever give a gift to a friend? Maybe you picked flowers or nuts or berries and shared them. You thought your friend would like your gift and say thanks. But instead, your friend grabbed the gift and ran off without saying anything. Did you know that's what we do to God sometimes? God is so good to us. He gives us his love, but we don't always thank him for it.

What does God give you? What should you give him?

DEAR GOD, you are very good to me. So I want to give you my thanks. In Jesus' name. Amen.

September 18

Giving in Love

[Jesus] said, ". . . This poor widow gave only two small coins. But she really gave more than all those rich people." LUKE 21:3

Jesus saw some rich people give money for God's work. They gave a lot, but they still had a lot left. Then he saw a poor woman give two little coins. Jesus said she gave more than the rich people. She showed her love for God by giving him everything she had.

Which is more important: How much money you give for God's work or how much love you give to God?

DEAR GOD, I'll give you as big an offering as I can. But most of all, I'll give you my love. Amen.

September 19

Wanting to Give

Give from what you have. If you want to give,
your gift will be accepted. 2 CORINTHIANS 8:11-12

Do you have a thousand dollars? Probably not!
God doesn't expect you to give him anything
you don't have. What's important to him is that you
want to give what you can. These are some things you may want to do
with your money: Help poor people. Buy things for your church. Help
missionaries travel far away to teach people about Jesus.

What is important to God about the way you give?

DEAR GOD, please show me how I can use
some of my money for your work. In Jesus'
name. Amen.

September 20

Don't Tell!

When you give to the poor, give very secretly. . . . Your Father can see what is done in secret, and he will reward you.
MATTHEW 6:3-4

Did you ever do something nice without telling anyone? That would be a good secret. Jesus tells us to keep it a secret when we give money to poor people. That doesn't mean you shouldn't tell your family. You just don't need to tell anyone else. God will know anyway and will do nice things for you.

Why is giving money to poor people a good secret to have?

DEAR GOD, when I do kind things, help me not to show off by telling everyone. Amen.

September 21

Plenty for Everyone

God . . . can give you all you need and more. Then there will be . . . plenty left over to give joyfully to others, too. 2 CORINTHIANS 9:8

When you take your offering money to church, are you happy to do it? Or do you wish you could keep the money? Maybe you think you need it to buy something for yourself. The Bible says that when you're happy to give what you can, God will give you all you need for yourself, too! He will even give you more than you need. Then you'll be able to keep on giving to others.

What does God do for you when you give to others?

DEAR GOD, thank you for helping me have everything *I* need when I help others have what *they* need. Amen.

September 22

A Reason for Waiting

You load the wagons with many crops. The pastures are full of sheep. . . . Everything shouts and sings for joy.
PSALM 65:11, 13

All year God sends sunshine and rain to help farmers' crops grow. In the fall the farmers load their crops onto wagons. They take the grain to places where it's made into food. God also gives farmers pastures of green grass. They can feed their animals there. The living things are so happy they seem to shout and sing!

Why does everyone want to shout and sing in the fall?

THANK YOU, THANK YOU, THANK YOU, GOD! I'm glad you make the farmers' crops grow so I can have food to eat! Thank you for animals in the pastures too. Amen.

September 23

Come to the Wedding!

There was a wedding in the town of Cana in Galilee. Jesus' mother was there. Jesus and his followers were also invited. JOHN 2:1-2

Do you know what happens at a wedding? A woman and a man get married! These two people want to become a family, so all their friends come to the wedding. Everyone is happy and has a good time.

Jesus and his mother and his friends all went to a wedding.

Would you like to look at some wedding pictures? Maybe your parents can show you pictures of their wedding.

DEAR GOD, thank you for happy weddings, when two people become one family. In Jesus' name. Amen.

September 24

Jesus, Please Help!

Jesus' mother said to him,
"They have no more wine."
JOHN 2:3

In Bible times weddings often lasted for a whole week! The wedding guests ate and drank and had a good time. The family that invited everyone had to be sure that there was enough to eat and drink. But at the wedding Jesus went to, the family ran out of wine. So there was nothing but water to drink. Jesus' mother felt bad for them, so she told Jesus about it. She just knew that he would be able to help.

What problem did Mary tell Jesus about?

DEAR JESUS, thank you for letting me come to you with my problems. Amen.

September 25

The Right Time

Jesus answered, "Dear woman, why come to me? My time has not yet come." JOHN 2:4

Mary knew that Jesus was not just an ordinary son. She knew that God had sent him. But other people didn't know that yet. Jesus hadn't done any miracles. He hadn't done special things that only God's Son could do. Now his mother wanted him to help a family have more wine for their wedding guests. But Jesus wasn't ready to let people know who he was yet.

Why didn't people know who Jesus was yet?

DEAR JESUS, thank you for knowing the right time for everything. Amen.

September 26

Do What He Says

[Jesus'] mother said to the servants,
"Do whatever he tells you to do."
JOHN 2:5

Mary knew that no matter what Jesus said, he would help in some way. So she talked to the servants. They worked for the family that invited everyone to the wedding. Mary told the servants to do what Jesus said. So when Jesus told them to fill some big jars with water, they did. When he said to give some to the man in charge of the party, they did.

What did Jesus ask the servants to do? Did they do it?

DEAR JESUS, I know that you tell me in the Bible about the things you want me to do. Help me to do what you say. Amen.

September 27

The First Miracle

The servants took the water to the master. When he tasted it, the water had become wine. JOHN 2:8-9

Did you ever take a drink that you thought was juice but turned out to be pop? Surprise! When the servants poured from the big jars, they thought they were pouring water. After all, that's what they had put into the jars. Surprise! Jesus had done a miracle—his first one! The man in charge liked the wine. But only the servants knew what Jesus had done.

What was the first miracle that Jesus did?

DEAR JESUS, thank you for letting me learn about your first miracle. You can do anything! Amen.

September 28

The Best for Last

The master of the wedding called the bridegroom and said to him, "People always serve the best wine first. . . . But you have saved the best wine till now." JOHN 2:9-10

A man who gets married is called a "bridegroom" or a "groom." At the wedding that Jesus went to, the man in charge had a happy message for the groom. He said that the new wine was even better than the wine that was served first! Neither of the men knew that Jesus had turned plain water into this good wine.

Why was the new wine so good?

DEAR JESUS, thank you for doing everything so well. Whatever you do is the best! Amen.

September 29

Power to Help

*In Cana of Galilee,
Jesus did his first
miracle . . . and his
followers believed in him.* JOHN 2:11

What a special wedding! Not only did everyone have a good time, but Jesus' friends learned who he was. They knew that only God's power could turn water into wine. Jesus, God's Son, had that power. He could do a miracle, and he did it to help people. He helped a family have plenty of good wine for their wedding guests. And he helped his friends believe in him.

What happened because of the miracle Jesus did?

DEAR JESUS, thank you for the power you have to do things no one else can do. Thank you for using your power to help people. Amen.

September 30

All New

*When someone becomes a Christian,
he becomes a brand new person inside.*
2 CORINTHIANS 5:17

Jesus told some servants to put water into special jars. What did Jesus do to the water inside the jars? He turned it into wine!

Jesus wants to change you on the inside too. When you learn to love and trust him, you become nice and new inside! You're happy, and you feel like doing good things.

How can you become a new person on the inside?

DEAR GOD, thank you for sending Jesus to make me a new and better person. Thank you for the way he helps me want to do what's right. In Jesus' name. Amen.

October 1

Don't Stop Now!

*We must not become tired of doing good. . . .
When we have the opportunity to help anyone,
we should do it.* GALATIANS 6:9-10

Do you make your bed, hang up your clothes, set the table, and put your toys away every day? Those are good things to do, so you shouldn't get tired of doing them. The Bible says that whenever you can, you should help others. That includes all of the people in your family!

What are some ways that you help at home?

DEAR GOD, when I get tired of doing good things, help me remember that you want me to keep doing them whenever I can.
In Jesus' name.
Amen.

October 2

Pleasing Everyone

Jesus continued to learn more and more and to grow physically. People liked him, and he pleased God. LUKE 2:52

When Jesus was a boy, he learned many new things, just like you! Perhaps his mother, Mary, helped him learn to sweep the floor and to play with other children. Joseph probably helped him learn to make things from wood. Jesus grew bigger, too, just like you! His neighbors liked him. And God, his Father in heaven, was pleased with him.

When Jesus was a boy, in what ways was he like you?

DEAR GOD, I want to please you just like Jesus did. In his name. Amen.

October 3

Listening

My child, listen to your father's teaching.
PROVERBS 1:8

Were you ever so busy playing or watching TV that you didn't hear what your mom or dad said? God wants you to listen to your parents! He has given them the job of teaching you the things they know. Maybe your dad will teach you how to do your best, how to get along with friends, and how to obey God. Whenever you're with your dad, listen carefully to him. He just may be teaching you something that God wants you to know!

When should you listen to your dad? What things have you already learned from him?

DEAR GOD, thank you for my dad. Help me to listen to him, especially when he teaches me about you. Amen.

October 4

Remembering

Do not forget your mother's advice.
PROVERBS 1:8

"Don't touch the hot stove." "Cover your mouth when you sneeze." "Share your toys." Does your mom give you advice like that? If you don't take her advice, what might happen? You might burn a finger on the stove. Your baby sister (or brother or friend) might catch your cold. You might get into a fight with a friend. God helps your mom give you good advice, doesn't he? And the Bible says that he wants you to remember what she says!

What are some things your mom has told you that you should remember to do?

DEAR GOD, thank you for my mom. Help me to remember the things she tells me. Amen.

October 5

A Happy Family

*The father of a good child
is very happy. . . . Make
your father and mother
happy. Give your mother
a reason to be glad.*
PROVERBS 23:24-25

Your mom and dad do a lot of things for
you, don't they? They earn money to buy the things you need. They
cook and wash and fix things. They teach you about God and tuck you in
bed. So what can you do for *them?* Can you listen to them and do what
they say? Can you give each of them a big hug and a kiss? Of course!
And then you can say, "I love you!"

How will you make your parents happy this week?

DEAR GOD, help me to show my mom
and dad that I love them. Amen.

October 6

Learning from Church Leaders

Follow the leadership of those who are older. I PETER 5:5

Did you ever play Follow the Leader? At church you have many leaders. Some of them are teachers, and some are helpers. But all of them are older than you, aren't they? The Bible says that you should let those older people lead you. That doesn't mean you have to walk or talk just like they do. It does mean that you should learn to love God and other people the way they do.

What can you learn if you let your Sunday school teacher be one of your leaders?

DEAR GOD, thank you for my Sunday school teacher and other leaders at my church. Amen.

October 7

How to Love

[Jesus said,] "Love each other as I have loved you." JOHN 15:12

When people say they love you, how do you know it's true? You can tell by the way they act, can't you? They give you hugs, they're kind to you, and they like to be with you. The things they do show that their words are true!

When Jesus lived on earth, he showed his love by helping people, doing kind things, and letting children spend time with him. Then he told us to love each other in the same way.

What are some ways you can show that you love someone?

DEAR GOD, thank you for sending your Son, Jesus, to show us how to love each other. In Jesus' name. Amen.

October 8

How Are You?

Enjoy other people and . . . you will grow to love them. 2 PETER 1:7

In the picture, some children are making fun of an older woman at church. Perhaps the people in the family will tell the children to stop. Maybe one of them will talk to the woman. She might look old and tired and cranky. But if the family members show that they care, she might have a lot to talk about. The family will enjoy listening and will learn to love the older woman.

Should you make fun of people or enjoy them?

DEAR GOD, thank you for all of the different kinds of people you have made. Help me to enjoy them and love them. Amen.

October 9

Friends Forever

[Ruth said,] "Every place you go, I will go." RUTH 1:16

Ruth loved Naomi. Ruth had been married to Naomi's son. But Naomi's son was no longer living. Neither was her husband. Now Ruth and Naomi were best friends. And they were a family. Ruth promised to stay with Naomi and go wherever she went. So the two women traveled together. They went to Naomi's hometown.

Maybe you can't always go where your friends go. Can you still pray for them? How else can you be kind to them?

DEAR GOD, thank you for my friends. I pray that you'll be with them wherever they are. In Jesus' name. Amen.

October 10

A Warm Welcome

The people of the island [of Malta]
were very kind to us. They made a bonfire
on the beach to welcome and warm us. ACTS 28:1-2

Paul and his friend Luke were in a boat that came apart in a storm. All of the people on the boat made it safely to an island. They were glad to get there because the island people were very friendly. It was cold and rainy. So the island people made a big fire to help everyone from the boat get warm.

How did the people on the island welcome everyone from the boat?

DEAR GOD, thank you for people who are nice to me when I need help. In Jesus' name. Amen.

October 11

Free Clothes

A woman named Dorcas . . . was a believer who always did kind things for others, especially the poor. ACTS 9:36

Dorcas liked to make clothes. But she didn't make them just for herself. She made them for others, especially people who were poor. If the people had no money, that was OK. They didn't have to pay Dorcas. Then Dorcas became very sick and died. Jesus' friend Peter prayed for her, and she came back to life again!

Are any of your clothes too small for you? Maybe you can give them to a poor person.

DEAR GOD, show me how to help poor people like Dorcas did. In Jesus' name. Amen.

October 12

Helping Jesus

*[Jesus said,] "I, the King . . . will say,
'. . . I was hungry and you fed me.
I was thirsty and you gave me
water.'"* MATTHEW 25:34-35

Someday everyone who loves
Jesus will see him on a throne in
heaven. He will tell us that we fed him
and gave him water. We'll wonder
when we did those things. He will say
that whenever we did kind things for
others, we did them for him, too.
Isn't that exciting?

*Can you help someone in your family who is thirsty? Can you
give money to buy food for hungry people? How will those
things help Jesus?*

DEAR JESUS, thank you for letting
me help you as I help the people
around me. Amen.

October 13

Many Ways to Be Kind

*I was alone . . . and you invited me
into your house. I was without clothes,
and you gave me something to wear.
I was sick, and you cared for me.
I was in prison, and you visited me.*
MATTHEW 25:35-36

Jesus will tell us someday about many kind things that we did for him. If we let a lonely person visit us, we're letting Jesus visit also. If we share our clothes, we're sharing with Jesus, too. If we're kind to a sick person, we're being kind to Jesus. And if people visit someone in prison, they're visiting Jesus.

What kind things can you do for Jesus?

DEAR JESUS, show me lots of ways to be kind to other people and to you. Amen.

October 14

Animal Friends

A good man takes care of his animals. PROVERBS 12:10

The Bible says we should take care of the animals God made. Zookeepers, farmers, and veterinarians take care of many different kinds of animals. A lot of people have pets. If you have a pet, you should take good care of it. Even if you don't have a pet, you can be kind to birds, bunnies, and other people's pets!

What are some ways you can be kind to animals?

DEAR GOD, thank you for all of the different animals you made. Thank you for the people who take care of them. Show me how I can help too. Amen.

October 15

A Fake God

*[Ahab] married Jezebel. . . . Then Ahab began
to serve Baal and worship him. He did more
things to make the Lord . . . angry than all
the other kings before him.* 1 KINGS 16:31, 33

Jezebel was a wicked queen. Instead of
worshiping God, she worshiped a fake god
named Baal. Jezebel got her husband, King Ahab,
to worship Baal too. They thought this fake god
would take care of them.   They thought it
would bring rain to make   crops grow
                              throughout their
                              country. But of course it couldn't.
                              Only God can do that.

What did Ahab and Jezebel do that was wrong?

DEAR GOD, I love you very much. Help me to
never stop loving you. In Jesus' name. Amen.

October 16

A Message from God

Elijah said to King Ahab, "I serve the Lord. . . . As surely as the Lord lives, I tell you the truth. No rain or dew will fall during the next few years unless I command it." I KINGS 17:1

Elijah was a prophet of God. He brought people messages from "the Lord," which is another name for God. Elijah gave Ahab and Jezebel a message they didn't want to hear. Elijah told them there wouldn't be any rain unless he said there would be. God had him give that message to the king and queen.

What message did Elijah give to the king and queen?

DEAR GOD, thanks for being a living God. I want to listen to messages from you in the Bible. Amen.

October 17

Safe by a Brook

The Lord spoke his word to Elijah: "Leave this place. Go east and hide. . . . I have commanded ravens to bring you food."
1 KINGS 17:2-4

Elijah was safe from the wicked king and queen. God told Elijah to hide by a brook, and God took care of him there. Elijah drank water from the brook. And he ate the food that big, black birds brought to him. God had the birds bring him bread and meat every morning and every evening.

How did God keep Elijah safe?

DEAR GOD, thank you for keeping Elijah safe. I'm glad you are more powerful than any wicked king or queen. Amen.

October 18

A Widow Will Help

The Lord spoke his word to Elijah, "Go to Zarephath in Sidon.
Live there. I have commanded a widow there to take care of you."
I KINGS 17:8-9

Soon there was no water left in the brook that Elijah was hiding by. He had no water to drink. So God sent him to another country. God said that a widow—a woman whose husband had died—would take care of him. When Elijah came to Zarephath, he saw a woman near the entrance to the town. He knew she was the one who would help him.

What did God do for Elijah in another country?

DEAR GOD, thank you for taking care of Elijah when the rain stopped and the brook dried up. Amen.

October 19

Bread for Everyone

*Elijah asked [the widow], "Would you
bring me a little water in a cup?
. . . Please bring me a piece
of bread, too."* 1 KINGS 17:10-11

Elijah asked for bread. But the widow said
she had no extra food. Well, Elijah told
the widow to bake bread for him anyway!
Then there would be enough flour and oil
to bake bread for her and her son, too. Elijah
said that God would see to it that the flour
and oil wouldn't run out. There would be
enough until the rain came and crops
began growing again. And that's just
what happened!

**When the widow helped Elijah,
what happened?**

DEAR GOD, I'm glad nothing
is impossible for you! Amen.

October 20

A Promise

Obadiah was in charge of the king's palace.
While Obadiah was walking along, Elijah met him. I KINGS 18:3, 7

God wanted Elijah to go and see King Ahab. God said that he was soon going to send rain. On the way, Elijah met Obadiah, one of the king's important helpers. Elijah said to tell the king he was there. Obadiah was afraid that Elijah might be gone by the time the king came out to see him. But Elijah promised that he wouldn't leave. And he didn't!

What promise did Elijah keep?

DEAR GOD, help me to do my best to keep my promises. In Jesus' name. Amen.

October 21

Meet Me on the Mountain

Elijah [said to King Ahab], ". . . You have not obeyed the Lord's commands. . . . Now . . . meet me at Mount Carmel. Also bring the 450 prophets of Baal there." 1 KINGS 18:18-19

It was time for Elijah to come out of hiding. He wanted people to know the real God. He didn't want them to keep worshiping the fake god, Baal. So God's prophet Elijah asked to have 450 prophets of Baal meet him at the top of Mount Carmel. They would pray and see who would answer—God or Baal.

Why was Elijah going to the top of a mountain?

DEAR GOD, thank you for people who want to help others know who you are. Amen.

October 22

The God Who Is Real

*Elijah . . . said, ". . . If the Lord is the true
God, follow him. But if Baal is the true God,
follow him!"* 1 KINGS 18:21

Elijah talked to the people who had come together on
Mount Carmel. He told them that they could not
keep on worshiping both the Lord and Baal. Both couldn't be God, so one
had to be a fake. The people would have to decide which one was the real
God. The people didn't know what to say. So they didn't say anything.

What did Elijah tell the people?

DEAR GOD, I know you are real because I can talk to you and you answer
my prayers. Thanks, God! Amen.

October 23

Who Will Answer?

You prophets of Baal, pray to your god. And I will pray to the Lord. The god who answers the prayer will set fire to his wood. He is the true God.

1 KINGS 18:24

Elijah said he would build a stone altar where he could worship the Lord. He would put wood on top of it. The prophets of Baal were to build an altar where they could worship Baal. Elijah knew that Baal could not hear any prayers. The people had just made him up. Elijah also knew that the Lord was the real God. The Lord *could* hear and answer prayer.

"The Lord" is another name for God. What did Elijah know about the Lord?

DEAR LORD, thank you for helping people know that you really are God. In Jesus' name. Amen.

October 24

No Answer

[The prophets of Baal] shouted, "Baal, answer us!" But there was no sound.

1 KINGS 18:26

The 450 prophets of Baal prayed from morning to evening. They worshiped their god by dancing around the altar they had built. They prayed louder, just in case Baal was sleeping or too busy to hear them. But Baal was a fake god. He wasn't even alive. He never had been! So there was no one to hear the prophets no matter how loudly they prayed.

Why couldn't Baal hear any prayers?

DEAR GOD, I pray that people who don't know you will learn that they can talk to you in your Son Jesus' name. Amen.

October 25

Fire from Heaven

*[Elijah prayed,] "Lord, answer my prayer.
Show these people that you, Lord, are God."*
1 KINGS 18:37

In the evening, Elijah built the altar of the Lord.
Three times he had the people pour water on
it. Then Elijah prayed. And the Lord sent fire
from heaven! It burned up the whole altar, even
the stones. The people knew that water is
what you use to put *out* a fire, not *start* one!
Only God could have started that fire.
So the people began to worship him.

How did the Lord show that he is God?

DEAR LORD, I praise you for the great God
you are. Amen.

October 26

Please Send Rain

[Elijah] got down on his knees. I KINGS 18:42

Sometimes when people pray, they get down on their knees. Elijah got down on his knees to talk to God about sending rain. God hadn't sent rain for a long time because he wanted his people to learn that Baal couldn't help them. As Elijah prayed, his helper saw dark clouds. Soon the rain came down. Now crops would begin growing again!

Why hadn't there been any rain for a long time?

DEAR GOD, I thank you for sending the sunshine and the rain. Thank you for knowing what we need. Amen.

October 27

You, Me, and God

There are many ways in which God works in our lives. But it is the same God who works in all of us. I CORINTHIANS 12:6

Elijah helped people learn that only one God answers prayers. Many years later, Paul also wanted people to know that there is only one God. So Paul wrote letters that we can read in the Bible. Paul said that God helps us do different things for him. You are good at one thing, and I'm good at something else. But it's God who helps us both!

Are you good at helping? being kind? giving? trusting Jesus?

DEAR GOD, thank you for the things you help me do for you. Amen.

October 28

Every Part Is Important

God . . . made many parts for our bodies. The eye can never say to the hand, "I don't need you." The head can't say to the feet, "I don't need you."
1 CORINTHIANS 12:18, 21

Is every part of your body important? Of course! Paul wrote that each part of your body has its own job to do. Then he said that's how it is with God's family. Each part of the family is important. Each person has a job to do. When we work together, we're one family with many parts!

Why is each person in God's family important?

DEAR GOD, I think it's great to be part of your family. Show me what I can do for you at my church. Amen.

October 29

Everyone Cares

If one part [of the body] suffers, all parts suffer with it. If one part is honored, all the parts are glad.
1 CORINTHIANS 12:26

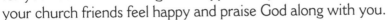

If your stomach hurts, your whole body feels sick. When your stomach gets better, your whole body feels good and you're happy again. That's how it is with God's family. If you feel sad, your church friends feel sad too. They want to hug you and pray for you. When something nice happens to you, your church friends feel happy and praise God along with you.

How do your church friends feel when you're sad? How do they feel when you're happy?

DEAR GOD, thank you for the way my church friends care about me. Amen.

October 30

You Really Should Do That

Encourage each other every day. HEBREWS 3:13

Sometimes people say, "I encourage you to do that." They're saying that something is a good idea. The Bible says that the people in God's family should encourage each other to do what's right every day! A long time ago, a boy whose last name was Wesley encouraged his friends. He did it by raising his hand to let everyone know he had prayed to God that day. Then some of his friends raised their hands to show that they wanted to pray too.

What can you encourage your friends to do?

DEAR GOD, thank you for the people who encourage me. Help me to encourage someone too. In Jesus' name. Amen.

October 31

One Rule

*The whole Law
can be summed up in
one command. It is,
"Love others as
you love yourself."*
GALATIANS 5:14

God gave us rules
called the "Law."
These rules help us to be
happy. The most important
rule is about love. Did you
know that you love yourself?
Well, you do! You show it by
the way you care about
yourself. You want people to be
kind to you, right? And you don't want anyone to laugh at you or hurt
you, right? God wants you to love others just as much.

What is God's most important rule for his family?

DEAR GOD, thank you for my friends. Help me to show that I love them.
Help me to care about them as much as I care about myself. Amen.

November 1

Four Seasons

There is a right time for everything. . . . There is a time to plant and a time to pull up plants.
ECCLESIASTES 3:1-2

Do you know what farmers and gardeners did last *spring?* They planted seeds! During the *summer,* the seeds grew into big plants. Now it's *fall,* isn't it? Farmers and gardeners have gathered fruit, vegetables, and grain from their plants. Soon it will be *winter.* Many farmers and gardeners will rest until they begin planting again next spring.

What do you like to do during each of the four seasons?

DEAR GOD, thank you for spring, summer, fall, and winter. Amen.

November 2

A Time to Be Born

*There is a time to
be born and a time to die.*
ECCLESIASTES 3:2

People look at puppies and say, "How tiny!" "How sweet!" "How cute!" When puppies are born, their eyes are closed and they sleep a lot. Soon they start to run around, chase things, and chew everything in sight! When they become grown-up dogs, they like to sit beside you and lick you. After many years they get old. They sleep a lot until it's time for them to die.

What do you like best about puppies? kittens? babies?

DEAR GOD, cute puppies make me happy. But I feel sad when an animal dies. I know you understand how I feel. Thank you, God. Amen.

November 3

Together with Jesus

*[Paul wrote,] "We do not want
you to be sad as others who have no
hope. . . . Because of Jesus, God will
bring together with Jesus those who have died."*
1 THESSALONIANS 4:13-14

Everyone's life on earth will come to an end someday.
That's good for people who love Jesus. Do you know why?
It's because they will live with him after they die. So even though we
feel sad when someone dies, we can still be glad that the person is with
Jesus. And we can be glad that we'll all be together again someday.

**What good thing will happen someday for people who
love Jesus?**

DEAR GOD, I'm glad that your Son, Jesus, came back to life after he died
so that we can do that too. In Jesus' name. Amen.

November 4

Tears and Giggles

There is a time to cry and a time to laugh. There is a time to be sad and a time to dance.
ECCLESIASTES 3:4

When you feel sad, it helps to cry, doesn't it? Maybe you cried when a friend moved away. Or when you saw a dead bird. Or when someone was unkind to you. When you feel sad, Jesus does too.

When you feel happy, you like to laugh, don't you? Maybe you laugh and skip and twirl around when you're having fun. When you feel happy, Jesus does too.

When do you cry? When do you laugh?

DEAR JESUS, I'm glad it's OK to cry when I feel sad and it's OK to laugh when I feel happy. Thanks for doing those things with me. Amen.

November 5

It's a Puzzle!

We know that in everything God works for the good of those who love him. ROMANS 8:28

Did you ever have a hard time figuring out how to put a puzzle together? Things that happen may be hard to figure out too. A friend might get very sick, or someone's parent might lose a job. Then we might say, "What a puzzle that is!" That means we don't understand why it happened. We may never figure it out. But we can be sure that God will work things out for our good. That's because he loves us and we love him!

What puzzling things have happened to you?

DEAR GOD, thank you for helping me trust you to bring good out of things I can't figure out. Amen.

November 6

Sad Now, Happy Later

We do not enjoy punishment. . . . But later . . . we have peace, because we start living in the right way. HEBREWS 12:11

When you do something bad, your parents won't let you get away with it. Why not? It's because they love you—it really is! They want you to please God. And even God himself will train you. He will keep you from feeling right about doing bad things. Then he will help you feel happy and peaceful when you do what's right.

How does being trained to do what's right help you?

DEAR GOD, thank you for training me to do what's right. Amen.

November 7

Good Things Are Coming!

[Jesus said,] "You might be laughed at and treated badly because you follow me. . . . Be very glad! For a great reward is waiting for you up in Heaven." MATTHEW 5:11-12

Kids who want to do bad things might not be nice to you. If they want to steal apples and you say no, they may make fun of you. You can be glad about that. After all, these things will happen for just a little while. Jesus says that if you love him, good things will be waiting for you in heaven. You'll live with Jesus forever!

When should you be glad to let someone make fun of you?

DEAR JESUS, I love you. And I'm glad about the good things that are waiting for me in heaven! Amen.

PRIVATE

November 8

God Never Leaves

[Paul wrote,] "I am sure that nothing can separate us from the love God has for us." ROMANS 8:38

Sometimes you and your dad have to go your separate ways, don't you? But while your dad is away, you know he still loves you. If he isn't too busy, he may call you or send you a message on the computer. With God it's even better. He never leaves you! Even though you can't see him, he always listens when you pray. There isn't one thing that can separate you from God's love!

How is God's love even better than your father's love?

DEAR GOD, thank you for your love. I'm glad you and I will never have to go our separate ways. Amen.

November 9

Someone to Comfort

[God] comforts us every time we have trouble, so that we can comfort others when they have trouble. 2 CORINTHIANS 1:4

Do you ever think no one understands how you feel? You can always talk to God, no matter if you're sad or lonely or afraid. God will comfort you, and you'll feel much better. Do you know what God wants you to do then? He wants *you* to comfort someone! It might be a friend, a little sister or brother, or even a pet!

After God comforts you, what does he want you to do?

DEAR GOD, thank you for all the times you've comforted me. Now help *me* find someone to comfort. In Jesus' name. Amen.

November 10

Safe with God

*The Lord protects you as the
shade protects you from the sun.*
PSALM 121:5

Have you ever sat under a big tree on a hot
day? The shade from the tree protects you
from getting hot and sunburned, doesn't it? The
Bible says that the Lord (another name for God)
protects you the way shade does. He keeps you
safe from bad things. He doesn't let anything bad
happen to you that he can't help you with.

What bad things might God protect you from?

DEAR LORD, thank you for protecting me.
I feel safe with you, just like I do when
I sit under a big tree. Amen.

November 11

Calling Jesus

[Bartimaeus] heard that Jesus . . . was walking by. The blind man cried out, "Jesus . . . please help me!" MARK 10:47

A blind man named Bartimaeus was begging people to give him money. Then he heard that Jesus was coming by. He knew that Jesus could give him more than money. Jesus could make his eyes see! Then he wouldn't need to beg anymore. Bartimaeus called to Jesus, and Jesus helped him. Jesus never turns away anyone who calls to him.

How did Jesus know that Bartimaeus wanted his help?

DEAR JESUS, thank you for listening whenever I tell you what I need. Thanks for answering, too! Amen.

November 12

Jesus Understands

When [Jesus] lived on earth, he was tempted in every way that we are, but he did not sin. HEBREWS 4:15

When Jesus was a young man, helping in the carpenter shop, he may have been tempted to say things he shouldn't. The Bible says he was tempted in every way that we are. So when we tell Jesus what we're tempted to do, we know he understands. The difference between Jesus and us is that we often do the bad things we're tempted to do. We sin. Jesus never did. As God's perfect Son, he can forgive our sins.

Why does Jesus understand what it's like to be tempted?

DEAR JESUS, thank you for understanding what it's like to be tempted. But I'm glad you never sinned. Amen.

November 13

A Good Time in Jail?

Paul and Silas were thrown into jail. The jailer . . . put them far inside the jail. He pinned down their feet between large blocks of wood.
ACTS 16:23-24

Paul and Silas were in jail for teaching others about Jesus. Their feet were pinned down, so they couldn't even walk inside the jail. It wasn't a good time for them, was it? But they made it a good time anyway. They sang praises to God! That showed that they trusted God to take care of their problem. He did—by sending an earthquake!

Why did Paul and Silas sing in jail?

DEAR GOD, when I'm not having a good time, help me to trust you anyway! In Jesus' name. Amen.

November 14

Friendly Help

*[Paul wrote,] "Epaphroditus
[ee-PAF-roh-DIE-tus] is my
brother in Christ. . . . When I
needed help,
you sent him to me."*
PHILIPPIANS 2:25

Paul was in jail
again. This time
he was by himself. He had
been in jail for a long time.
Some of Paul's church friends
sent a man with a
very long name to help him!
Epaphroditus brought him money and helped to cheer him up. Do you ever
need to be cheered up? Maybe your mom can invite a friend from church
to come over. A friend can play with you and make you laugh!

How can church friends help each other?

DEAR GOD, thank you
for my friends at
church. Thank you
for friends who help
to cheer me up.
Amen.

November 15

Big Troubles and Little Troubles

Help each other with your troubles. GALATIANS 6:2

Some troubles are little. Maybe your family can't afford to buy the computer game you want. So a friend lets you play the game at her house. Some troubles are big. Maybe you break your leg. So your family and friends help you during the whole time that you use crutches.

The children in the picture had big troubles. Soldiers came to their African village and set fire to their homes. So they had to find another place to live.

What does God want you to do when someone has trouble?

DEAR GOD, thank you for people who help me with my troubles. Show me how to help my friends. Amen.

November 16

Trusting Jesus

We who are strong in faith should help those who are weak. ROMANS 15:1

Do you ever feel afraid at night? Your room gets dark, you are alone, and you begin to cry. Perhaps you have older brothers or sisters who come into your room to comfort you. Or maybe your mom comes. Or your dad. Their faith is strong. They have loved Jesus for a long time, and they trust him. They know he is with you and will take care of you. So they help you believe that also.

Name someone you can help as your faith in Jesus grows stronger.

DEAR GOD, thanks for the people who help me when I forget to trust you and my faith is weak. Help me to trust you more and more each day. In Jesus' name. Amen.

November 17

Just like Mom

[God said,] "I will comfort you as a mother comforts her child."
ISAIAH 66:13

When you feel sad, you can run into your mom's arms! She always understands, doesn't she? She holds you close and lets you cry as long as you want to. Then she wipes your tears away and maybe gives you a cookie!

That's the kind of love God gives. You won't feel his arms around you or get a cookie from him. But you can talk to him, and he will make you feel happy again—even if your mom isn't around.

How is God like your mother?

DEAR GOD, I really like to tell you about the things that make me feel sad. You understand and help me feel better. Thank you, God! Amen.

November 18

Storms

A fierce storm came up on the lake. . . . [Jesus] spoke to the storm. "Quiet down," he said. And the wind and waves stopped and all was calm! LUKE 8:23-24

Storms can be scary, can't they?

Jesus was sleeping in a boat one time when a storm came up. Jesus' friends were afraid, but he just told the storm to stop. And it did!

A stormy night may seem like a bad time for you, but it can become a good time if you trust Jesus. You can talk to him, and he will help you fall asleep.

What kinds of storms do you have where you live? Rain? Snow? Wind? Can you trust Jesus in any storm?

DEAR JESUS, help me to trust you to take care of me whenever there is a storm. Amen.

November 19

God Will Go with Me

Be strong and brave. . . .
The Lord your God will be
with you everywhere you go.
JOSHUA 1:9

For a long time, Moses was the leader of God's people. Then God chose Joshua to be the next leader. His job was to take the people into a new land. God told Joshua to be "strong and brave." God didn't just say that and leave. He promised to be with Joshua everywhere he went. That promise is for you, too! You can be brave everywhere you go because God will go there with you.

Can you name some places where you'll go this week? Who will go with you?

DEAR GOD, thank you for going with me everywhere. I won't be afraid. I'll be brave! Amen.

November 20

A River to Cross

They stepped into the water. Just at that moment, the water stopped flowing. . . . They crossed the Jordan River on dry land. JOSHUA 3:15-17

Joshua and the people had to cross a river that was deep and wide. It looked very scary. But Joshua knew that many years ago God had split a big sea. Moses and the people had walked across on dry land. Now Joshua told the people that God wanted them to start crossing the river. As soon as they did, the river stopped flowing! Everyone walked across on dry land.

What did God do for Joshua and the people?

DEAR GOD, thank you for taking care of Joshua and the people. Thank you for taking care of me. Amen.

November 21

A City for God's People

*Joshua was near Jericho.
He looked up and saw a man
standing in front of him. . . .
The man [said,] ". . . I have
come as the commander of the
Lord's army."* JOSHUA 5:13-14

Joshua and the people were now in the land where God wanted them to live. But soon they came to a city with thick, high walls around it. The people in the city didn't want Joshua and his people to live there. So what was Joshua going to do now? As he came near the city, he saw a man who said he was the leader of God's army. How exciting! Joshua was getting help from heaven!

Why did God send special help to Joshua?

DEAR GOD, thank you for knowing when I need you and for sending the help I need. Amen.

November 22

The Best Plan

The Lord said to Joshua, ". . . Your army is to walk around the city once a day for six days. . . . On the seventh day you are to walk around the city seven times. As you walk, the priests shall blow their trumpets. . . . All the people are to give a mighty shout. And the walls of the city will fall down." JOSHUA 6:2-5

God told Joshua just how to get into the city of Jericho, didn't he? It wasn't the kind of plan Joshua would have come up with on his own. But he knew that God's plan would work. So he told the people to do what God said.

Why was God's plan better than any plan Joshua might have had?

DEAR GOD, help me to remember to talk to you whenever I need to know what to do. Amen.

November 23

The Walls Tumble Down

At the sound of the trumpets and the people's shout, the walls fell. And everyone ran straight into the city. JOSHUA 6:20

Every day for six days, Joshua and the people marched around the city of Jericho. On the seventh day, they blew their trumpets and shouted. They did everything God had told them to do. And everything happened just as God had said it would. The thick, high walls began to crack and crumble. And God's people got out of the way as the walls tumbled down with a loud crash!

What happened when the people did what God said?

DEAR GOD, thank you for helping me when I obey you the way Joshua and the people did. Amen.

November 24

Don't Forget to Love God!

The Lord your God fights for you, as he promised to do. So you must be careful to love the Lord your God. JOSHUA 23:10-11

Many years had gone by since the walls of Jericho tumbled down. Now Joshua was old, but he talked to God's people one more time. He told them to remember how God kept his promise to help them. God did his part by fighting for them. Now the people were to do their part. They were to love God! If they did, they would be very careful to obey him and not forget him.

What did God do for his people? What were the people to do for God?

DEAR GOD, you do so many things for me. Help me to be careful to show my love for you. Amen.

November 25

You're Awesome, God!

How great [God] is! His power
cannot be stopped! His understanding has no limits.
PSALM 147:5

Just think about some of the awesome things that God does. He feeds the birds and the butterflies. He sends clouds and sunshine. He makes the snow fall on the tops of the mountains. Then he sends warm weather to make the grass and the flowers grow. On top of all that, he understands us and helps us when we trust him! He is happy when we trust him to love us and care for us. God is wonderful, isn't he?

What are some awesome things God does? What are some things you trust God to do for you?

DEAR GOD, I praise you for being so great. Help me trust you to always love and care for me. Amen.

November 26

I'm Amazing!

You made all the parts of my body. . . .
Thank you for making me so wonderfully!
It is amazing to think about!
PSALM 139:13-14

Before you were born, God formed your body inside your mother. He gave you bones and muscles to help you stand, run, and lift things. He gave you a brain so you can think. He gave you a heart and lungs so you can breathe. And he put skin over your whole body. God also gave you hair for your head and nails to protect your fingers and toes. It's amazing how he thought of everything!

What do you think is the most amazing thing about your body?

DEAR GOD, thank you for the wonderful way you made me— inside and out! Amen.

November 27

God's Power and Love

Those who go to God Most High for safety will be protected by God All-Powerful.
PSALM 91:1

God not only made you—he loves you! You can trust him to keep you safe because he wants to do it and he has the power to do it. The girl in the picture fell down, but she only scraped her knee. God kept her safe from being hurt worse than that. He knew her mother could help with the hurt knee. And he will make it heal up quickly so she can run and play again. He's an awesome God!

Why can you trust God to keep you safe?

DEAR GOD, thanks for taking care of me and for helping me to heal up quickly when I hurt myself. Amen.

November 28

Taking Time to Pray

Early the next morning, Jesus woke and left the house while it was still dark. He went to a place to be alone and pray. MARK 1:35

When Jesus lived on earth, he always found time to talk to God and ask him what to do. One time Jesus was staying at Peter's house, helping people who were sick. The next morning, Jesus got up so early that it was still dark! He missed his Father in heaven and wanted to pray by himself. You can pray by yourself too! God is glad when you take time to talk to him.

Did Jesus think it was important to talk to God? How do you know?

DEAR GOD, help me to remember that I can talk to you anytime, even when I'm all by myself. Amen.

November 29

Talking Things Over

*Jesus went off to a mountain to pray. . . .
The next morning, Jesus called his followers to
him. He chose 12 of them.* LUKE 6:12-13

Jesus was going to choose 12 of his followers to be his special helpers. He wanted to be sure to choose the right ones. So Jesus went up on a mountain one evening to talk it over with his Father in heaven. He talked to God for a long time. The next morning, Jesus knew which 12 men he was going to choose. So he called his followers together and told them who the 12 would be.

What did Jesus do after he talked to God on a mountain?

DEAR GOD, I'm glad I can talk to you whenever I need to decide what to do. Thanks for helping me know what's right. Amen.

November 30

Doing What God Wants

*[Jesus prayed,] "Father, if it is
what you want, then let me not
have this . . . suffering. But do
what you want, not what I want."*
LUKE 22:42

Jesus went to a garden with his
special helpers one evening. He knew that he would soon be put on a
cross to die. He talked it over with God, his Father in heaven, just as he
always talked things over with God. Jesus told God that he didn't want to
suffer. But then Jesus said to God, "Do what *you* want, not what *I* want."

Jesus didn't want to suffer, but what did he say to God?

DEAR GOD, there are some things I wish I didn't have to do. But please
do what *you* want, not what *I* want. Amen.

December 1

Coming Again

Then people will see [Jesus] coming in clouds with great power and glory. MARK 13:26

Do you use an Advent calendar while you wait for Christmas? You can lift one flap every day. Maybe the pictures remind you to celebrate Jesus' birthday at Christmas. When Jesus came to earth as a baby, that was his first coming—his first advent. When Jesus comes back in the clouds as a grown-up, that will be his second coming. It will be more exciting than Christmas!

When do we celebrate Jesus' first coming? What will his second coming be like?

DEAR JESUS, thank you for Christmas. It helps me remember that you came to earth a long time ago. I'm glad that you're coming back! Amen.

December 2

An Exciting Time

[Jesus] will send his angels all around the earth. They will gather his chosen people from every part of the earth. MARK 13:27

It's exciting to think about the time when Jesus was born. We read about angels in the sky and shepherds in the fields and animals in the stable. But when Jesus comes back, there will be angels everywhere! It will be an even more exciting time than when Jesus was born! The angels will gather all of God's people together to be with Jesus. Won't that be wonderful?

What will angels do when Jesus comes back?

DEAR JESUS, I want to be with you when you come back to earth. I want to live with you forever! Amen.

December 3

Waiting

[Jesus said,] "No one knows when that day or time will be. . . . Only the Father knows. Be careful! Always be ready!" MARK 13:32-33

If your mom has to go away, you want to know when she's coming back, don't you? You want to be ready to give her a big hug!

After Jesus was born, he grew up and lived on earth for a while. Then he died on a cross and came back to life again. After that, he went back to heaven. He tells us that only God, his heavenly Father, knows when he's coming back again. So he wants us to always be ready. He could come back anytime!

Who knows when Jesus is coming back?

DEAR JESUS, I wish I knew when you were coming back. But I'll wait for you until you get here! Amen.

December 4

Work While You Wait

[Jesus said,] "My coming is like a man who went on a trip to another country. He laid out his employees' work for them to do while he was gone."
MARK 13:34

When the owner of a big house in Bible times went away, he would give his helpers work to do. And they would do everything he had asked them to do. Jesus said he is like the man who went away, and we're his helpers. This is the work Jesus has given us to do: We are to teach others about him and do kind things for one another. We are to love Jesus and obey him.

What can you do for Jesus while you wait for him to come back?

DEAR JESUS, help me to love you and to do kind things every day. Amen.

December 5

I'm Ready!

*The whole Bible . . . makes us well prepared
and fully equipped to do good to everyone.*
2 TIMOTHY 3:16-17

If you want to make a snowman, you'll need to wear your snowsuit, boots, and mittens. Maybe you'll find a carrot for a nose, buttons for eyes, and red gumdrops for a mouth. Then you'll be prepared for the weather and fully equipped to make a snowman! Learning what the Bible says prepares you for something too. You'll be ready to do good things when you learn what God wants you to do.

Can you name some Bible people whose stories have helped you learn to do good things?

DEAR GOD, thank you for Bible verses and stories that prepare me to do good things for people. Amen.

December 6

A Lot of Love

Live a life of love.
Love other people
just as Christ loved us. EPHESIANS 5:2

The Bible says to love others the way Jesus loves you. Well, Jesus loved you a lot to leave heaven and come to earth for a while. So that means you should love other people a lot. You can show your love by doing kind things. And that shouldn't just be at Christmas. You're to "live a life of love." That means to love others all day, every day, for as long as you live!

How can you show love for others at Christmas? How can you do it the rest of the year?

DEAR JESUS, thank you for *your* love and for all the people you've given *me* to love. Amen.

December 7

Pray for Leaders

Pray for kings and for all . . . leaders.
I TIMOTHY 2:2

It's easy to pray for people we love. We care about them and know what they need. But the Bible tells us to pray for our leaders also—police officers, firefighters, kings, presidents, and more. We may not know who all of these people are. But we know that they are in charge. And we know that they need a lot of wisdom to lead our country.

Who are some leaders that you can pray for?

DEAR GOD, I pray for the leaders in my town and in my country. Show them what to do every day. In Jesus' name. Amen.

December 8

Pray for Peace

Pray for the leaders so that we can have quiet and peaceful lives.
I TIMOTHY 2:2

Angels praised God and sang about peace on earth when Jesus was born. If we want peace in our world, we should pray for our leaders to help us have it.

Maybe it is quiet and peaceful where you live. You can pray that your leaders will help to keep it that way. For countries where there is fighting and war, pray that God will show the leaders how to bring peace soon.

How can your prayers help people in other countries?

DEAR GOD, please bring your love and peace to countries everywhere. Amen.

December 9

Friends Forever

[Paul wrote,] "I ask God, the Father of our Lord Jesus Christ, to give you wisdom. Then you will see and understand who Christ is."
EPHESIANS 1:17

Paul told people that he prayed for them. He prayed that they would know who Jesus is. Christmas is a good time to pray for people who don't care about Jesus. You can pray that they will listen to Christmas carols about him. You might also want to pray that they will go to church and learn about Jesus. You could send a Christmas card with a note that says you're praying.

How should you pray for friends who don't know much about Jesus?

DEAR JESUS, I pray that all of my friends will learn more about you this Christmas. Amen.

December 10

A Job for Jonah

The Lord spoke . . . to Jonah . . . : "Get up, go to the great city of Nineveh and preach against it. I see the evil things they do." JONAH 1:1-2

Jonah lived many years before Jesus was born. God had plans for Jonah, and God had plans for his Son, Jesus. But Jonah didn't cooperate the way Jesus did many years later. Jonah's job was to go and preach in the city of Nineveh. He didn't want to do it because the people there were enemies of God's people. So Jonah got on a boat that sailed away from Nineveh.

When God asked Jonah to go to Nineveh, what did Jonah do?

DEAR GOD, help me not to run away from the things you want me to do. Amen.

December 11

A Storm

[Jonah] found a ship that was going to the city of Tarshish. Jonah paid for the trip and went aboard. . . . But the Lord sent a great wind. . . . So the ship was in danger of breaking apart. JONAH 1:3-4

When it gets windy, big waves form on the water. The boat that Jonah was on was small. So it "was in danger of breaking apart." The sailors were afraid. They began throwing things into the water so the boat would be lighter and wouldn't sink. Jonah was asleep the whole time!

God wanted Jonah to go to Nineveh, not Tarshish. So what did God do?

DEAR GOD, thank you for being in control of everything, even the wind and the waves. Amen.

December 12

A Storm Ends

[The sailors] knew Jonah was running away from the Lord. . . . So the men said to Jonah, "What should we do to you to make the sea calm down?" JONAH 1:10-11

Jonah told the other men in the boat to throw him into the water. He knew that God would make the wind stop blowing then. The men didn't want to do it, but the storm got worse. So they threw Jonah out of the boat. The wind stopped, and the men worshiped God!

What were two good things that happened after the sailors threw Jonah out?

DEAR GOD, thank you for making good things happen even when everything seems to be going wrong. Amen.

December 13

Inside a Big Fish

The Lord caused a very big fish to swallow Jonah. Jonah was in the stomach of the fish three days and three nights. JONAH 1:17

Throwing Jonah out of the boat was good for the sailors. But was it good for Jonah? Well, it didn't seem that way at first! But God had a job for Jonah, and he was going to help Jonah do it. God saw to it that a big fish swallowed Jonah! The fish was so big that Jonah was safe inside it for three days and nights!

How did God take care of Jonah?

DEAR GOD, thank you for taking care of people in ways that no one else would even think of. Amen.

December 14

Jonah and God

Then the Lord spoke to the fish. And the fish spit Jonah out of its stomach onto the dry land. JONAH 2:10

While Jonah was inside the big fish, he thanked God for saving him. He also said he would keep all of his promises to God. That pleased God. So he told the fish to spit Jonah out and put the man on dry land. Then Jonah was safe, both from the storm and from the big fish!

What did Jonah say to God from inside the fish? What did God do for Jonah?

DEAR GOD, I don't ever want to have to talk to you from inside a fish! But I thank you for hearing me wherever I am. Amen.

December 15

A Second Chance

Then the Lord spoke . . . to Jonah again. The Lord said, "Get up. Go to the great city Nineveh. . . ." So Jonah obeyed the Lord.
JONAH 3:1-3

The first time God told Jonah to go to Nineveh, Jonah ran away. Or at least he tried to! The second time God told Jonah to go there, Jonah obeyed. The people of Nineveh didn't love God. So God had a sad message for them. Jonah gave them the message. It said that after 40 days the city would no longer be there.

Why do you think Jonah didn't want to go to Nineveh at first?

DEAR GOD, thank you for helping Jonah do something that wasn't easy. Thanks for helping me, too, when I have to do things that aren't easy. Amen.

December 16

A Whole City Is Sad

The people of Nineveh believed in God. . . . They put on rough cloth to show how sad they were. JONAH 3:5

In Bible times people put on rough, scratchy cloth when they were sad. Well, everyone in the whole city of Nineveh was sad about the message Jonah brought them from God. The people believed in God and were sorry about the bad things they had done. The king told everyone in the city to stop doing bad things.

What did the people of Nineveh do when they heard God's message?

DEAR GOD, I'm sorry about the bad things I've done. I need your help to stop doing those bad things. In Jesus' name. Amen.

December 17

Jonah Is Angry

God saw what the people did. He saw that they stopped doing evil things. So God . . . did not punish them. JONAH 3:10

God was pleased. Jonah had finally gone to Nineveh. The people there weren't doing bad things anymore. They were sorry, and God forgave them. He didn't get rid of their city.

Jonah should have been pleased too. But he wasn't. He was angry. Jonah thought that the people of Nineveh should have been punished. He didn't think God should have been so kind to them.

Why was God pleased? Why was Jonah angry?

DEAR GOD, sometimes my friends seem to get away with the bad things they do. Help me to be glad that you forgive them just as you forgive me. Amen.

December 18

The Plant

The Lord made a plant grow quickly up over Jonah. . . . The next day . . . God sent a worm to attack the plant. Then the plant died. JONAH 4:6-7

Jonah was sitting near Nineveh, waiting to see what would happen. While he sat there, God made a plant grow over him. Jonah liked the shade. But the next day God sent a worm to eat up the plant. Then it died, and Jonah sat in the hot sun. Jonah felt sorry for himself. He was very upset.

Do you ever feel sorry for yourself? When?

DEAR GOD, I don't understand everything you do. But help me to always believe that what you do is right. Amen.

December 19

God's Love

The Lord said, "You showed concern for that plant.
But you did not plant it or make it grow. . . . Then
surely I can show concern for the great city Nineveh."
JONAH 4:10-11

God knew that Jonah was upset about the plant. So God talked to him about it. God said that Jonah didn't have anything to do with making the plant grow. If Jonah cared so much about the plant, why shouldn't God care about Nineveh? He did care! He cared about the people in the city. He cared about the animals, too!

God loved the people of Nineveh long before they loved him.
What does that tell you about God?

DEAR GOD, thank you for your love. I'm glad you care about everyone, even me! Amen.

December 20

Coming Soon!

God sent the angel Gabriel to [Mary]. The angel said to her, "Don't be afraid, Mary, because God is pleased with you. Listen! . . . You will give birth to a son, and you will name him Jesus." LUKE 1:26, 30-31

In five days we're going to celebrate Jesus' birthday! Many months before Jesus was born, God sent an angel to Mary. She was very surprised. Mary was even more surprised when she heard the angel's message from God! She must have been afraid, too, because Gabriel told her she didn't need to be.

What was God's message to Mary?

DEAR GOD, thank you that the Bible tells us all about the time when your Son, Jesus, was born. Amen.

December 21

I'll Do It!

Mary said, "I am the servant girl of the Lord. Let this happen to me as you say!" Then the angel went away. LUKE 1:38

When Mary heard the angel's message, she wondered what it meant. Gabriel explained that Mary was going to be the mother of God's very own Son, Jesus! Mary knew this wouldn't be easy because people wouldn't understand. But she told the angel that she would be God's servant. She would do whatever God wanted her to do.

What did Mary agree to do? Why?

DEAR GOD, thank you that Mary did what you wanted her to do. Help me to do the things you want me to do. Amen.

December 22

A Husband for Mary

An angel of the Lord came to [Joseph] in a dream. The angel said, ". . . Don't be afraid to take Mary as your wife. The baby in her is from the Holy Spirit." MATTHEW 1:20

Joseph heard that Mary was going to have a baby. He didn't know what to do because he wasn't the father. But God wanted Joseph to take care of baby Jesus. So God sent an angel in a dream. The angel said that Mary's baby came from the Holy Spirit of God. The angel said that it was OK for Joseph to let Mary be his wife. So he did!

What was God's message to Joseph?

DEAR GOD, thank you for helping Joseph believe your message. Help me to believe what you say in the Bible. Amen.

December 23

A Long Trip

The emperor of Rome . . . made a law that all the people should be counted. Everyone was told to go back to the home of his ancestors to be registered. LUKE 2:1, 3

Joseph and Mary lived in the town of Nazareth. But King David had been born in Bethlehem. He was one of Joseph's *ancestors*, a relative who had lived many years before. So Joseph and Mary had to go to Bethlehem to be counted. The trip seemed very long to Mary, who was going to have her baby soon.

Why did Joseph and Mary go to Bethlehem?

DEAR JESUS, thank you that it's almost time to celebrate your birthday. Amen.

December 24

A Place to Stay

There were no rooms left in the inn.
LUKE 2:7

Have you ever taken a trip? Maybe you stayed in a cabin or at your grandma's house or at a motel. In the town of Bethlehem there was an inn for travelers. It had many rooms, but the rooms were filled with people when Mary and Joseph came. The only place left for them to stay was a stable. That's where the animals stayed. So Mary and Joseph had to go where their donkey went!

Why couldn't Mary and Joseph stay at the inn?

DEAR GOD, I'm glad Mary and Joseph found a place to stay, even if it was just a stable. Amen.

December 25

The Best Gift

The time came for [Mary] to have the baby. . . . She wrapped the baby with cloths and laid him in a box where animals are fed.
LUKE 2:6-7

Mary and Joseph were spending the night in a stable. They didn't get much sleep because that was the night when Jesus was born! Mary wrapped baby Jesus in strips of cloth, as all mothers did in Bible times. Then she laid him in a manger. This wooden box was where the animals usually ate hay. What an exciting night for everyone, including the animals!

Whose birthday are you celebrating today? But who is getting presents?

DEAR GOD, thank you for sending a very special Gift to the world—your very own Son, Jesus! Amen.

December 26

Great News from Heaven

That night, some shepherds were in the fields nearby watching their sheep. An angel of the Lord . . . said to them, ". . . Today your Savior was born in David's town." Then a very large group of angels from heaven joined the first angel.
LUKE 2:8-11, 13

Sheep were sleeping in a field near Bethlehem. Their shepherds thought it was an ordinary night. That was before the angel came! With bright light all around, the angel told the shepherds about baby Jesus, the Savior. Then more angels came, and they all praised God.

What news did the shepherds hear? Who brought the news to them?

DEAR GOD, I praise you for sending baby Jesus. Amen.

December 27

The First Visitors

The shepherds went quickly and found Mary and Joseph. And the shepherds saw the baby lying in a feeding box. LUKE 2:16-17

When the angels left, did the shepherds think they had just been dreaming? No! They knew that God had sent the angels and that a special baby had been born. So they hurried into town, found the baby, and told everyone about the angels. Then they went back to their sheep, praising God. They were so happy that they had found baby Jesus!

What did the shepherds do about the good news they heard?

DEAR JESUS, I'm glad that you grew up and went back to heaven. I can't see you like the shepherds did, but I can talk to you whenever I want to. Thank you! Amen.

December 28

Out-of-Town Guests

Some wise men . . . asked, "Where is the baby who was born to be the king of the Jews? We saw his star in the east. We came to worship him." MATTHEW 2:1-2

Some wise men lived far away from the place where Jesus was born. When they saw a new star, they knew that a king had been born. So they traveled to Jerusalem and talked to King Herod. He sent them to Bethlehem. Herod said to let him know when they found the king because he wanted to worship the new king too. But Herod was telling a lie. He really was jealous of the new king.

How did the wise men know there was a new king?

DEAR GOD, thank you for letting people from far away know about baby Jesus. Amen.

December 29

Gifts for a Little King

*The same star they had seen in the east . . .
went before [the wise men] until it stopped
above the place where the child was.*
MATTHEW 2:9

The wise men still didn't know exactly where
they were going. So they were happy to see again the star that they
had been following. It took them all the way to a house in Bethlehem.
When they saw little Jesus there, they got down on their knees and
worshiped him. They gave him gold and two kinds of very nice perfume.

What did the wise men do when they saw Jesus?

DEAR JESUS, the wise men didn't know much about you, but they
worshiped you. I know a lot about you, so of course I want to worship
you too! Amen.

December 30

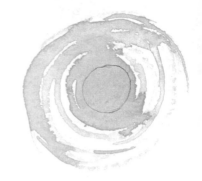

Don't Go That Way

*God warned the wise men in a dream not
to go back to Herod. So they went home to
their own country by a different way.*
MATTHEW 2:12

When you travel, you might see a detour sign. That means you have to take a different road. Maybe a bridge is out, and you would be in danger if you kept going. Well, God knew there was danger ahead—not for the wise men, but for Jesus. King Herod wanted to hurt Jesus. God told the wise men not to go back to Jerusalem and see the king again. So the wise men found a different way to go back home.

How did God keep his Son, Jesus, safe?

DEAR GOD, thank you for keeping Jesus safe. And thanks for all the times when you keep me safe. Amen.

December 31

One Rule

When the baby was eight days old, he was . . . named Jesus. . . .
[Then] the time came for Mary and Joseph to . . . present him
to the Lord. LUKE 2:21-22

No one in the Bible is more important than Jesus! That's the name the angel said to give him. It's a special name that means "Savior." Jesus came to be our Savior—to save us from our sins. When he was a month old, Mary and Joseph presented him to God at the temple. Jesus came from God, his heavenly Father. And as he grew up, he lived his life on earth for God.

What is special about the name "Jesus"?

DEAR GOD, thank you for sending Jesus to be my Savior. I want to live for God just like he did. Amen.